ON THE
JOB
SERIES

REAL PEOPLE WORKING *in*

ENTERTAINMENT

Jan Goldberg

VGM Career Horizons
NTC/Contemporary Publishing Group

Library of Congress Cataloging-in-Publication Data

Goldberg, Jan.
　　Real people working in entertainment / Jan Goldberg.
　　　　p.　　cm.—(On the job series)
　　Includes bibliographical references.
　　ISBN 0-8442-6569-1 (cloth).—ISBN 0-8442-6570-5 (paper)
　　1. Performing arts—Vocational guidance.　2. Entertainers—
Interviews.　I. Title.　II. Series.
　　PN1580.G57　　1998
　　791′.023—dc21
　　　　　　　　　　　　　　　　　　　　　　　　　　98-17060
　　　　　　　　　　　　　　　　　　　　　　　　　　CIP

This book is dedicated to the memory
of a dear aunt—Estelle Lefko

Published by VGM Career Horizons
A division of NTC/Contemporary Publishing Group, Inc.
4255 West Touhy Avenue, Lincolnwood (Chicago), Illinois 60646-1975 U.S.A.
Copyright © 1999 by NTC/Contemporary Publishing Group, Inc.
Printed in the United States of America
International Standard Book Number: 0-8442-6569-1 (cloth)
　　　　　　　　　　　　　　　　　　　　0-8442-6570-5 (paper)
98　99　00　01　02　03　VL　6　5　4　3　2　1

791.023
G618

Contents

Acknowledgments   vii

How to Use This Book   ix

Introduction to the Field   xi

1. Careers in Acting   1

Overview   1

Training   2

Job Outlook   3

Salaries   4

Related Fields   5

Interview: Jennifer Aquino, Actress   5

Interview: Gonzo Schexnayder, Actor   8

Interview: Jack Stauffer, Actor   10

Interview: Joseph Bowman, Actor   12

Interview: Mike Matheson, Voice-Over Talent   14

Interview: Richard Koz, Television Personality   19

Interview: Joe Hansard, Actor   23

For More Information   25

2. Careers in Music and Dance   27

Overview   27

Training   30

Job Outlook   33

Salaries   34

Related Fields   36

Interview: Mark Marek, Singer and
Band Owner   37

Interview: Ed Goeke, Music Director   38

Interview: Priscilla Gale, Opera Singer   40

For More Information   **42**

3. Careers in Radio and Television   47

Overview   **47**

Training   **48**

Outlook   **50**

Salaries   **50**

Related Fields   **51**

Interview: Sylvia Perez, Television
News Anchor   51

Interview: Carol Stein, Radio Talk-
Show Host   53

Interview: Brian R. Powell, Radio
Personality/DJ   56

Interview: Chuck Woodford, Radio
Show Host   60

Interview: Robin Truesdale, Television
News/Video Editor   61

For More Information   **64**

4. Careers Behind the Scenes in Music and Acting   67

Overview   **67**

Training   **74**

Job Outlook   **75**

Salaries   **76**

Related Fields   **78**

Interview: Ross Norton, Stage Manager,
Lighting Systems Technician   79

Interview: Randall Presswood, Director of
Performing Arts Facilities   83

Interview: Dennis Parichy,
Lighting Designer   89

Interview: Twyla Mitchell, Costume Shop
Teaching Assistant, Stage Manager   94

Interview: Mark T. Simpson,
    Lighting Designer   97
Interview: David Palmer, Theater Manager   100
For More Information   **103**

5. **The Business of Entertainment**   **105**

Overview   **105**

Training   **111**

Job Outlook   **112**

Salaries   **113**

Related Fields   **115**

Interview: Brian J. Swanson, Company
    President and Agent   115

Interview: Wayne Keller,
    Artists' Representative   116

Interview: Bill Hibbler, Company Owner
    and Artist Manager   119

Interview: Gary Murphy, Publicist   125

For More Information   **127**

About the Author   **131**

Acknowledgments

The author gratefully acknowledges

- The numerous professionals who graciously agreed to be profiled in this book

- My dear husband, Larry, for his inspiration and vision

- My children, Deborah, Bruce, and Sherri, for their encouragement and love

- Family and close friends—Adrienne, Marty, Mindi, Marshall, Cary, Michele, Paul, Michele, Alison, Steve, Marci, Steven, Brian, Jesse, Bertha, Uncle Bernard, and Aunt Helen for their faith and support

- Diana Catlin for her insights and input

- Betsy Lancefield, editor at VGM, for making all projects rewarding and enjoyable

How to Use This Book

On the Job: Real People Working in Entertainment is part of a series of career books designed to help you find essential information quickly and easily. Unlike other career resources on the market, books in the *On the Job* series provide you with information on hundreds of careers, in an easy-to-use format. This includes information on

- The nature of the work

- Working conditions

- Employment

- Training, other qualifications, and advancement

- Job outlooks

- Earnings

- Related occupations

- Sources of additional information

But that's not all. You'll also benefit from a firsthand look at what jobs are really like, as told in the words of the employees themselves. Throughout the book, one-on-one interviews with dozens of practicing professionals enrich the text and enhance your understanding of life on the job.

These interviews tell what each job entails, what the duties are, what the lifestyle is like, what the upsides and downsides are. All of the professionals reveal what drew them to the field and how they got started. And to help you make the best career choice for yourself, each professional offers you some expert advice based on years of experience.

Each chapter also lets you see at a glance, with easy-to-reference symbols, the level of education required and salary range for the featured occupations.

So, how do you use this book? Easy. You don't need to run to the library and bury yourself in cumbersome documents from the Bureau of Labor Statistics, nor do you need to rush out and buy a lot of bulky books you'll never plow through. All you have to do is glance through our extensive table of contents, find the fields that interest you, and read what the experts have to say.

Introduction to the Field

Some people seem to be "born entertainers"—grabbing brushes to use as microphones from the time they are very young. Any audience will do—parents, relatives, neighbors, sisters and brothers, cousins, aunts, friends, acquaintances, school classmates, and anyone else who is willing to listen and/or watch. Other people develop an interest in entertainment slightly later in life—realizing the joy and enlightenment brought to those who are spectators.

If you are reading this book, you are probably one of the people I described above. The book will provide you with a number of options and offer you some understanding of what it is like to work in the field of entertainment.

All of the careers outlined in this book have some factors in common, but they are nevertheless distinctly different. Read through the chapters to hone in on the differences, and pay special attention to the interviews of individuals who are working in the field. They will provide you with special insights about the day-to-day life of performing that job. As you are perusing the book, ask yourself the following questions:

- How much time, energy, and money am I willing to devote to prepare myself for this career?

- Will I be able to take the disappointments that are bound to be a part of pursuing a career in entertainment?

- Do I have a true zest for performing for others— or in aiding in the performances?

- Am I willing to accept the fact that there might not be large monetary compensations?

- Do I understand the fact that I might not become one of the bigger stars in Hollywood?

- Do I want a nine-to-five job or am I willing to work longer hours?

- Am I willing to work in whatever physical surroundings are necessary?

- Am I persistent—even in the face of failures?

- How well do I work under pressure? How well do I handle stress?

- Am I able to work well as part of a team?

- Do I have strong communications skills?

- Am I willing to travel to promote my career?

- Am I a patient and resilient professional?

- Can I adapt to the stress of not having long-term job security?

This book will provide valuable information on working conditions and lifestyles so that you can make good choices based upon reliable facts.

Although *On the Job: Real People Working in Entertainment* strives to be as comprehensive as possible, not all jobs in this enormous field have been covered or given the same amount of emphasis. If you still have questions after reading this book, there are a number of other avenues to pursue. You can find more information by contacting the sources listed at the end of each chapter or locate professionals to talk to and observe as they go about their work. Any remaining gaps in your understanding of a particular occupation can be filled by referring to the *Occupational Outlook Handbook.*

CHAPTER **1** Careers in Acting

EDUCATION
B.A. or B.S. recommended

SALARY/EARNINGS
$1,400 and up

OVERVIEW

Actors express ideas and create images, based on a script, in theaters, film, television, and radio. They "make the words come alive" for their audiences.

Actors entertain and communicate with people through their interpretations of dramatic roles. Only a few actors achieve recognition as stars on the stage, in motion pictures, or on television. A somewhat larger number are well-known, experienced performers, who frequently are cast in supporting roles. Most actors struggle to "break into" the profession and pick up parts wherever they can. Many successful actors continue to accept small roles, including commercials and product endorsements. Some actors employed by theater companies teach acting courses for the public. In addition to the actors with speaking parts, "extras," who have small parts with no lines to deliver, are used throughout the industry.

Acting demands patience and total commitment, because there are often long periods of unemployment between jobs. While under contract, actors are frequently required to work long hours and to travel. Evening work is a regular part of a stage actor's life. Flawless performances require tedious memorizing of lines and many repetitious rehearsals. On television, actors must deliver a good performance with very little preparation. Actors need stamina to withstand the heat of stage or studio lights; the heavy costumes; long, irregular hours; and adverse weather conditions that may exist on location. When plays are on the road, traveling is necessary. Actors often face the anxiety of intermittent employment and frequent rejections when auditioning for work.

TRAINING

Aspiring actors and directors should take part in high school and college plays or work with little theaters and other acting groups for experience.

Formal dramatic training or acting experience is usually necessary, although some people enter the field without it. Most people take college courses in theater, arts, drama, and dramatic literature. Many experienced actors get additional formal training to learn new skills or improve old ones. Training can be obtained at dramatic arts schools in New York and Los Angeles, and at colleges and universities throughout the country offering bachelor's or higher degrees in dramatic and theater arts. Most college drama curriculums include courses in liberal arts, stage speech and movement, directing, playwriting, play production, design, and history of drama, as well as practical courses in acting.

The best way to start building an acting career is to use local opportunities and then move on from there. Local and regional theater experience may help in obtaining work in New York or Los Angeles. Modeling experience may also be helpful. Actors need talent, creative ability, and training that will enable them to portray different characters. Training in singing and dancing is especially useful. Actors must have poise, stage presence, the ability to affect an audience, plus the ability to follow directions. Physical appearance is often a deciding factor in being selected for particular roles.

Many professional actors rely on agents or managers to find work, negotiate contracts, and plan their careers. Agents usually earn a percentage of an actor's contract.

As actors' reputations grow, they work on larger productions or in more prestigious theaters. Actors also advance to lead or specialized roles. A few actors move into acting-related jobs—as drama coaches or directors of stage, television, radio, or motion picture productions. Some teach drama in colleges and universities.

The length of a performer's working life depends largely on training, skill, versatility, and perseverance. Some actors, directors, and producers continue working throughout their lives; however, many leave the occupation after a short time because they cannot find enough work to make a living.

To become a movie extra (also known as a *background artist*) one must usually be listed by a casting agency, such as Central Casting, a no-fee agency that supplies all extras to the major movie studios in Hollywood. Applicants are accepted only when the number of persons of a particular type on the list is less than the foreseeable need. In recent years, only a very small proportion of the applicants have succeeded in being listed.

JOB OUTLOOK

Employment of actors, directors, and producers is expected to grow at a faster rate than for most occupations through the year 2005. Rising foreign demand for American productions, combined with a growing domestic market—fueled by the growth of cable television, home movie rentals, and television syndications—should stimulate demand for actors and other production personnel. However, the large number of people desiring acting careers and the lack of formal entry requirements will probably continue to create keen competition for acting jobs. Only the most talented will find regular employment.

Growth of opportunities is expected both in recorded media and in live productions. More and more people who enjoy live theatrical entertainment will continue to go to theaters for excitement and aesthetics.

Touring productions of Broadway plays and other large shows are also providing new opportunities for actors. However, employment may be somewhat affected by government funding for the arts. A decline in funding could dampen future employment growth in this segment of the entertainment industry.

SALARIES

Minimum salaries, hours of work, and other conditions of employment are covered in collective bargaining agreements between producers of shows and unions representing workers in this field. The Actors' Equity Association represents stage actors; the Screen Actors Guild (SAG) and the Screen Extras Guild cover actors in motion pictures, including television, commercials, and films; and the American Federation of Television and Radio Artists (AFTRA) represents television and radio performers. Any actor or director may, of course, negotiate for a salary higher than the minimum.

According to limited information, the minimum weekly salary for actors in Broadway stage productions is $1,000. Players in small, off-Broadway theaters receive minimums ranging from $380 to $650 a week, depending on the seating capacity of the theater. For shows on the road, touring actors receive about $100 per day (*per diem*) more for living expenses.

Actors usually work long hours during rehearsals. Once the show opens, they have more regular hours, working about thirty hours a week.

According to the SAG, motion picture and television actors with speaking parts earn a minimum daily rate of about $500, or $1,750 for a five-day week. Those without speaking parts, "extras," earn a minimum daily rate of about $100. Actors also receive contributions to their health and pension plans and additional compensation for reruns.

Earnings from acting are low because employment is so irregular. The Screen Actors Guild reports that the average income its members earned from acting is $1,400 a year, and 80 percent of its members earned less than $5,000 a year from acting. Therefore, many actors must supplement their incomes by holding jobs in other fields.

Some well-known actors have salary rates well above the minimums, and the salaries of the few top stars are many times the figures cited, creating a false impression that all actors are highly paid. Many actors who work more than a set number of weeks a year are covered by their union's health, welfare, and pension fund, including hospitalization insurance, to which employers contribute. Under some employment conditions, Actors' Equity and AFTRA members have paid vacations and sick leave.

RELATED FIELDS

People who work in occupations requiring acting skills include dancers, choreographers, disc jockeys, drama teachers or coaches, and radio and television announcers. Others working in occupations related to acting are playwrights, scriptwriters, stage managers, costume designers, makeup artists, hair stylists, lighting designers, and set designers.

INTERVIEW
Jennifer Aquino
Actress

Jennifer Aquino studied theater and dance at the University of California in Los Angeles (UCLA) and received a Bachelor of Arts in economics. As a member of the dance team, she was a UCLA Cheerleader for three years. In addition to cheering for UCLA's football and basketball teams, she also entered national dance-team competitions.

How Jennifer Aquino Got Started

"I grew up in Cerritos, California, and received my first taste of acting at St. Linus elementary school in Norwalk, where I played the leading role of the Princess in *Beyond the Horizon.*

Happily, I received the Performing Arts Award while attending Whitney High School.

"Following my college graduation, I got my first break playing Eolani, the wife of Dr. Jacoby in David Lynch's television series *Twin Peaks* (a result of my very first audition!). Then I got an agent and joined the Screen Actors Guild. I have been performing in various theatrical productions and am a founding member of Theatre Geo, as well as an active member of Theatre West and the East-West Players Network. (Watch for me in a national commercial for Ford trucks!)

"My television credits include 'Weird Science: The Paranormal Borderline,' *Fresh Prince of Bel Air, Santa Barbara,* and *Twin Peaks.*

"Films I've been in include *The Party Crashers, Prisoners of Love,* AFI's *It Makes You Wonder . . . How a Girl Can Keep from Going Under,* UCLA's *Fleeting Vanities of Life,* USC's *Unexpected Love,* and NYU's *Free Love.*

"And my theater credits include *People Like Me* at the Playwrights Arena; *Gila River* at the Japan America Theatre and at Scottsdale Center for the Arts in Arizona; *Cabaret* and *Sophisticated Barflies* at East-West Players; the PAWS/L.A. Gala Benefit at the Pasadena Playhouse; the STAGE Benefit at the Luckman Theatre; *The Really Early Dinner Theatre for Kids* at The Hollywood Playhouse; *Boys' Life, Hold Me!, Scruples,* and *Watermelon Boats* at Theatre West; *Mistletoe Mews* at Theatre Geo; and *Is Nudity Required?* at Playhouse of the Foothills.

"I remember performing at family gatherings ever since I was a small child. I always enjoyed being in the spotlight. To me, acting is like a child's game of pretend, something I have always enjoyed. I see it as a career where you can earn a lot of money while having a lot of fun. At the same time, you are entertaining people, impacting them, making them think, helping them to feel certain emotions, educating them, and helping them escape from their current lives.

"Most actors who are starting out hold some kind of side job, day job, or part-time job. For me, it was a career in the health-care industry working for Kaiser Foundation Health Plan. Then I became a health-care consultant for one of the big-six accounting firms, Deloitte & Touche LLP. I was such a good employee that my managers were flexible and would let me go out on auditions.

"After a few years, I realized that I was working too many hours (seventy to eighty per week), and I finally had to make a decision to quit my day job and focus 100 percent of my time on acting. After booking a few jobs, including a national commercial, I was able to do so. It was a big risk, but one I felt was necessary to take. I remember what my acting coach would say, 'Part-time work gets part-time results.' The more I put into acting, the more I got out of it."

What the Job's Really Like

"Don't be fooled—acting . . . is a lot of hard work! I am at it seven days a week, mornings, afternoons, evenings, weekends (forty to sixty hours per week). And if I'm not working on the creative side of acting (which is doing my homework for a job that I booked or for an audition), I am working on the business side of acting—talking to my agents, managers; networking; sending my head shots to casting directors, producers, directors, writers; attending seminars; meeting people, and so on. I also try to keep my stress level down and take care of myself by getting enough sleep, exercising, eating healthy, and having some relaxation time. And I have been fortunate—the sets I've worked on have all been positive experiences for me.

"What I like most about my work is that I can say that I am making a living doing what I absolutely love to do, and that I am pursuing my passion in life. Not too many people in this world can say that. What I like least about my work is that there are a lot of politics in it. It's not always the best actor who gets the job. Some of the time it's a certain look, what your credits are, who you know, and so forth that determine who gets the job. A lot of things are out of your control. That's just part of the business, and you have to accept it."

Expert Advice

"I would advise anyone who is considering acting as a career to pursue your dreams and be persistent—but only if it's something you absolutely love to do and there's nothing else in the world you would rather do. Pursue the creative as well as the business side of acting. Don't let anyone stop you from doing what you want to do. And always keep up your craft, by continuing your training."

INTERVIEW
Gonzo Schexnayder
Actor

Gonzo Schexnayder earned a bachelor's degree in journalism and advertising at Louisiana State University in Baton Rouge, Louisiana. He attended various acting classes at LSU and at Monterey Peninsula College in Monterey, California. He also attended Chicago's Second City Training Center for more than a year and then the Actors Center. He is a member of SAG and AFTRA.

How Gonzo Schexnayder Got Started

"I had always wanted to do stand-up comedy but didn't pursue it until graduating from college, when I began working with an improvisational comedy group. Four months later, the military sent me to Monterey, California, for language training. While there, I did my first staged reading and my first show. I'd never felt such elation as when I performed. Nothing in my life had given me the sheer thrill and rush that I experienced by creating a character and maintaining that throughout a given period of time. Nothing else mattered but that moment on stage, the other actors, and the scene we were performing.

"After completing the language program in November of 1990, I returned to Baton Rouge. There I began the long process of introspection about my career choices and what I wanted to do. I began to audition locally and started reading and studying acting. I still had not made the jump to being an actor; I was merely investigating the possibility.

"One night, while watching an interview with John Goodman, I realized how important acting had become to me. I knew that it possibly meant a life of macaroni and cheese, but I also knew that up until that moment, nothing had made me as happy or as motivated. While I believe I had the skills and the drive to make it in advertising (or whatever career I chose), I decided that acting was my only logical choice."

What the Job's Really Like

"Whether it's rehearsing a show, performing improvisation in front of an audience, or even auditioning for a commercial, it's fun. If you can separate the sense of rejection most actors feel for not getting a part, auditioning for anything becomes your job. Rehearsing becomes your life. Just as a carpenter's job is building a house, as an actor I look at my job as building my performance. The final product is there for me to look at and admire (if executed well), but the path to that product is the thrill.

"Unfortunately, I'm not at a point in my career where I'm making enough money to quit my day job. I'm close, but not close enough. I still feel the need to have some sense of financial stability or I lapse into thinking about money. It's all about balance and deciding what's really important. Sure, I'd love to have an apartment with central air and a balcony. I'd love to have a car that is still under warranty. But I know that by putting my efforts and money into my acting career, those other things don't matter. What matters is how it makes me feel. Cars and apartments don't give me the satisfaction that being an actor does.

"How many hours and how busy I am depends on what I'm doing. Over the last year I've worked with five other actors to open our own theater, Broad Shoulders Theatre, and have found my time constrained. On top of that I have been pursuing (with some success) a voice-over/on-camera career, in addition to working a full-time job. Yesterday I finished six days of shooting on a graduate-thesis film, and last weekend we opened our first show (TheatreSports/Chicago—improvisational comedy) at our new theater. We have another opening (which I'm not performing in) tonight, and we expect to open four more shows in the next three months. I've also taken a year of guitar classes and maintained my presence in acting and on-camera classes and workshops. I'm always busy and continually looking for the next chance to market myself and increase my salability as an actor (train, study, perform, work).

"I love the process of acting and sometimes just the fast-paced, eclectic nature of the business. There is always something new to learn and something new to try. The sheer excitement of performing live is amazing, and the personal satisfaction of getting an audience to laugh or cry simply by your words and actions is very gratifying."

Expert Advice

"There are many people who take advantage of an actor's desire to perform. Because acting is one of the only professions where there is an abundance of people willing to work for nothing, producers, casting directors, agents, or managers who only care about the money will take advantage of and abuse actors for personal gain. Being an astute actor helps prevent much of this, but one must always be on the lookout.

"I would advise others who are interested in this career to work where you are. Perfect your craft. Move when you *have* to—you will know when it's time. And, above all, trust your instincts."

INTERVIEW
Jack Stauffer
Actor

Jack Stauffer, a graduate of Northwestern University, has been a working actor since 1968. He created the role of Chuck Tyler in the popular television daytime drama *All My Children* and remained in that role for three and a half years (386 shows). Other regular television appearances include *Battlestar Galactica* and *The Young and Restless.* Episodic television appearances include *Lois and Clark, Viper, Designing Women, Quantum Leap, Perfect Strangers, Growing Pains, Knotts Landing,* and *Dynasty.* In all, he has appeared in forty prime-time television shows and numerous movies-of-the-week and miniseries. He was also costar in the movie, *Chattanooga Choo Choo.* He had parts in the theater versions of *My Fair Lady* and *Oliver!* at the Grove Theatre in San Bernadino County. Other play productions include *Annie Get Your Gun, Fiorello, Can Can, The Music Man, Mister Roberts,* and *Guys and Dolls.* His achievements also include parts in more than 200 commercials.

How Jack Stauffer Got Started

"I started as a child actor, but really didn't become a professional until I graduated from college in 1968. I simply sold my car, moved to New York, and hit the pavement!

"I grew up in the industry. My mother worked for Warner Brothers and was W. C. Fields's radio producer. My father produced the *March of Time* for radio during WWII. He then founded his own advertising agency and was responsible for many early television series in the days when the ad agencies had tremendous creative input into a television show. Many notable celebrities used to spend time in our living room. For as long as I can remember I have always wanted to be a performer. It has been my burning desire, despite my parents' best efforts to dissuade me from the vagaries of the industry. They would have been happy for me to pursue a more stable and lucrative career."

What the Job's Really Like

"Unless you are on a series or are a celebrity, you are constantly battling the belief that you will probably never work again. Thus, your workday consists of looking everywhere and calling anyone who might give you a job. Once you have done all you can do, you inevitably wait for the phone to ring. The vast majority of the time, it doesn't. So, most actors have other jobs—temporary work or selling or, in my case, teaching tennis—anything to make enough money to pay the bills so you can pursue your craft. When you are finally hired for a day or a week or a month or whatever it might be, every moment in your day suddenly has purpose. You get to do what you were meant to do, even if it is only for a short time or if the part is minuscule. You are on top of the world. Then it is over, and it is back to square one.

"The best thing about your work is the work itself. An actor lives by his emotions and his ability to convey them to an audience. A good actor makes it look easy even though it is very hard. That is why so many actors work for free. It is the work that fulfills them. Of course, if you get paid, it is much better. The recognition factor is important also. That is why so many actors return to the stage—the gratification is immediate. Any actor who says the applause means nothing to him is probably lying.

"The worst thing about the industry is that absolute lack of tenure. You are only as good as your next job. Your history, experience, and so forth don't mean much. This is because there is no studio system any more. With no continuity, it is difficult to slowly work your way up the ladder of success. The easiest way to get hired today is to have the executive producer of a hit show as your brother-in-law."

Expert Advice

"If you have an absolute, undying, uncontrollable passion to do this—and I mean that you will die if you don't—then by all means give it everything you have got. But if you are the slightest bit timid or unsure, choose another career. This is a business based on rejection, and it can destroy you. If you sell cars and somebody doesn't buy one, they simply don't want that car. As an actor, when you are turned down, they don't want *you*. It's difficult *not* to take it personally. You have to be very strong to keep at it."

INTERVIEW
Joseph Bowman
Actor

Joseph Bowman is an actor in the Los Angeles area. He is a high school graduate who has some college, vocational, and military training. He also participated in the Vanguard Theatre Ensemble Training Program for four years. He considers himself at the beginning of his acting career.

How Joseph Bowman Got Started

"I was in the Marine Corps for six years and attained the rank of sergeant via meritorious promotion. I thoroughly loved the United States Military Corps. It tended to reward a person who acted as if he enjoyed that kind of life, and I was such a person. It seems that I have always been able to act appropriately in any given situation. Older people usually find me charming. Younger people usually find me cool. I love to be the chameleon.

"Five years ago, a friend was attending a model-talent showcase that piqued my interest. I ended up doing it, and he didn't. Even though it was a fiasco, it had revived in me my love of performing."

What the Job's Really Like

"At my present level, I do a lot of background work. My military experience gets me a lot of work in productions that have a need for people who have 'been there' to add a flavor that normal actors don't always possess. Much of this work involves firing military weapons (blanks) and the knowledge of the safety concerns therein.

"There are not many typical days in acting because every production is very different. It is like working for a different company in a different capacity every day. I may be asked to simply put on a costume and chat (mime) with another actor for eight hours one day. Another day, I might be asked to put on the full battle-dress uniform of a branch of the military and fire an M-16 at a monster that isn't there! It varies widely, and that is why I love it.

"The hours and working conditions also vary greatly. Typically, jobs consist of ten-hour days with pleasant working conditions. Sometimes a shoot can be as quick as three hours, and

sometimes thirteen! It all depends on what the director is looking for and when he or she sees it.

"I enjoy being involved in the artistic side of life. I love
the people who populate the arts. They are intelligent, funny,
and varied. Nine-to-five has never been my style. I languish
and fade under fluorescent light, but shine a spotlight
my way . . . ahhh, and watch me grow ten feet tall and bul-
let proof.

"I most enjoy the variety and the opportunity to become a
character. I have worked my share of day jobs, and I hated the
monotony of them. Fame is not my goal. Riches are not my
goal. I simply want to do what I love and get paid for it. That
is my dream.

"The only thing I don't like about acting is that there is a lot
of classism. If you are on a shoot as a background actor, many
do not afford you the level of treatment that featured or lead
actors enjoy. It is simply a fact of life. Most actors at a high
level do not act snobbish to the lowest-rung actors, but many of
the production people do."

Expert Advice

"Study the craft and art of acting as if your life depended on it.
Enjoy life, and experience it to the fullest, because good artists
bring all their life experiences to their art. Don't let anyone
tell you that you are a fool for following your dream. Would
you rather be in your rocking chair, saying to yourself, 'I wish
I had at least tried' or 'I gave it my best shot, and had fun along
the way'?"

INTERVIEW
Mike Matheson
Voice-Over Talent

Mike Matheson earned a Bachelor of Science degree in psychology from Lawrence University in Appleton, Wisconsin. He has
earned his livelihood as a full-time freelance voice-over talent
since 1985.

How Mike Matheson Got Started

"I've always had an outgoing, performing kind of personality so this profession seemed natural to me. I've come to understand the fact that what I have is a gift, for which I am very appreciative.

"My background includes studying various musical instruments—piano, drums, saxophone, guitar—with private teachers. Then I performed in folk groups and rock bands during high school, singing and playing guitar. While attending college I first worked in radio at a college station, where I learned the basics of on-air work, production, commercial writing, and voice-overs. Then I worked as a professional musician (bass, guitar, vocals), performing in clubs throughout the Midwest, playing in folk, rock, jazz, country, and 'oldies' groups. Next, I worked in a small-market cable TV station (Janesville, Wisconsin) in every imaginable capacity. These were definitely the dues-paying years. In the two years at the station, I functioned as a talk-show host; sports anchorman and play-by-play; advertising salesman; producer, writer, and voice-over for commercials; camera operator; and telethon host. I can only describe this stage of my career as a real eye-opener—a true learning experience. But it gave me a great deal of perspective regarding what was to come.

"I then worked for a small-market radio station as program director, disc jockey, commercial producer, and voice-over, and I did my first freelance work for a handful of clients as commercial writer, producer, and voice-over.

"Subsequently, I relocated to Indianapolis and worked as a recording engineer in a studio specializing in commercial production. At the same time, I continued to expand my freelance voice-over work. When the freelance income surpassed my salary as an engineer, I decided it was time to step out on my own."

What the Job's Really Like

"Today, about 90 percent of my work is actually done in Chicago, where I moved in 1988. Actually, my employers are all over the country, but the work itself is done in Chicago recording studios. There are several studios in the Michigan Avenue area of downtown Chicago that do voice-over recording, as well as music and video production, all within about a mile radius of the major advertising agencies they serve. I occasionally work in suburban studios in Evanston and Oak Park. In rare instances, when the client cannot travel to Chicago or refuses to do the recording via telephone, I do the recording out of town. However, one of the advantages of living in Chicago is that most out-of-town employers would rather work in Chicago, traveling here, sometimes combining business and pleasure.

"Ironically, what I do is actually very basic. I talk on radio and TV commercials (as well as for industrial films and tapes). My voice is heard over the picture portion of television spots. It's recorded in a studio, after I have been selected (either from a demo tape, audition, previous employment, or word of mouth) and hired (via my agent) by an ad agency who has requested my voice. I read from a script and am directed by a producer or copywriter who has written the script. In the case of television work, I read either to a video that has already been assembled or 'cold,' without the picture. My voice, the music, and the sound effects are then edited to the picture to complete the commercial. Very seldom do I see or hear the finished product when my part of the job is done, either in television or radio, unless I happen to see or hear it on the air. This can be frustrating, and it would be much more satisfying if I could see what I'd contributed to the completed commercial. Then I wouldn't feel so detached from the creative process.

"There really is no typical day for me. Because of that, it is really up to me to give my day-to-day existence some structure and discipline. The need to keep an even keel is, to me, the single most important aspect of my job. That is because of the unstable and volatile nature inherent in this field. There is very little predictability in the amount of work, income, required time, or stress level—or in the personalities—involved in my work. That can be both good and bad. The variety can be very stimulating as well as stressful.

"My work can be extremely lucrative (a definite plus). With some national commercials, as few as eight or ten hours a week in the studio can be sufficient to earn a handsome living. A vast majority pay much less, however, and because of the occasional big payoff, the field is extremely competitive. For that reason, extensive (and expensive) marketing is a must. Seventy-five to eighty percent of my workweek is spent outside the studio, either doing auditions or promotion and marketing. If I get one job in fifteen or twenty auditions, I'm doing extremely well against the several hundred people competing in the Chicago market. To promote myself I do the following:

1. Send two to three mass mailings a year to 2,500 creatives (writers, producers, creative directors) at ad agencies in about ten Midwestern markets. All are custom designed and written, either by me or freelancers I hire. Because agency personnel is constantly changing, updating these mailing lists is an ongoing job.

2. Produce a voice demo tape or CD (it's my resume) annually and send copies to the same 2,500 people. This involves collecting copies of commercials I've done, assembling, and editing them into a two-minute sample of my work. I personally finance the production, duplication, and on-stage expenses of the tape as well as the mailers.

3. Pay a personal representative to make visits and calls on my behalf. With the number of voice-overs in the market, keeping contact with potential employers is a must.

"During an average week, I spend up to fifteen hours (maybe seven or eight sessions) in the studio in recording, and another three or four in auditioning. The upside of this, at first glance, is lots of free time. However, I have to be available on a moment's notice during regular work hours (forty to fifty hours a week). My time is my own only until someone needs me for work or an audition.

"Adaptability is an absolutely essential trait, and long-term planning is sometimes impossible. Making good use of free time is very important because I never know when it might end. That time is spent working on promotion and staying informed about my industry by reading trade papers or networking with other voice-overs, producers, recording engineers, and so on.

"The pace is hectic—and unpredictable. There's a lot of hurry-up-and-wait going on. Some weeks I may have only one audition and no sessions. I must wait and, at the same time, be prepared to be at a session immediately. So it can be slow one minute and very busy the next. Other weeks, I may have four sessions on Monday, then nothing until my Friday afternoon audition. In either case, sessions and auditions are very seldom booked more than a day or two ahead of time.

"Depending how busy one is doing sessions and auditions, this career can be either relaxed or stressful. It is most relaxing when there is a slow but steady stream of sessions and auditions—a condition that almost never exists! Perhaps the most unsettling part of the job is its unpredictability. Being extremely busy can be hectic and stressful, but preferable to and certainly less stressful than no work and no income.

"Sessions themselves can also range from a relaxed atmosphere, perhaps with a producer and client you like and know well, to very stressful—with many personalities (writer, producer, account executives, client, engineer, other voice-overs) and egos, many of whom you may not know involved. You may have the wrong voice for the job. Or you may be ill. Or you may simply have an off day. You've auditioned and been hired and paid to do well. If you don't, you probably won't work for that producer, agency, or client again. When you have a bad day, it makes them look bad.

"It's hardly ever physically dangerous. The most dangerous thing is if something were to happen to prevent me from working. If I don't work, I don't earn. If I became disabled, private disability insurance wouldn't begin to replace my earnings. There are no paid vacations. If I leave town, I might miss work that could potentially pay thousands of dollars. Learning to relax on vacations is a real art. I have to put lost income out of my mind so I can enjoy my time away.

"The other danger is that my voice will somehow go out of style—that whatever people like about it will no longer be in demand. I've accepted that I really have no control over that. I've learned that all I can do is continue to remind people I'm available, give it my best when I'm called, and save my money when the big jobs come along because, as one recording engineer said to me at the end of a recording session, 'you're fired again.' In some ways that sums up my existence as freelance voice-over. Every time I finish a job, I'm unemployed again and in search of the next one.

"When I am hired for a job, I take great satisfaction in knowing that I've beaten the best in the business to get that job. High risk—high payoff. The financial rewards pale in comparison to the joy I experience doing what I love. I feel blessed to have this job . . . one I am proud to say I do well. I love what I do. And, in spite of some of the pitfalls, I wouldn't trade it for any job in the world.

"A friend in the voice-over business says he feels like a thief. He fears that earning a living this way might be outlawed. He says that he's sometimes hesitant to answer his door. He's afraid the police may come to arrest him."

Expert Advice

"I'd advise others to keep your seat belt fastened. Keep your shirt on. Keep your sense of humor. Keep your ego in check. Don't take anything personally—especially rejection. Keep your head. And when you make money, keep it. Remember when you're working, you're making more than anyone in the room. Make their job easy. Make them look good.

"Enjoy it. You're lucky."

INTERVIEW
Richard Koz
Television Personality

Rich Koz has spent his entire broadcasting career in the Chicago area. Born in Chicago, he grew up in the northwest suburbs, getting his first taste of broadcasting at WMTH-FM, the radio station at Maine East High School in Park Ridge. While attending Northwestern University, Rich sent comedy material he had written to DJ and television personality Jerry G. Bishop, who was, at that time, portraying the original Svengoolie at Channel 32 in

Chicago. Bishop was so impressed by Rich that he took him on as writer and voice-talent for *Svengoolie.* When the program was canceled in 1973, Bishop brought Rich along to WMAQ radio as producer-writer "second banana" on his WMAQ-AM morning show.

How Richard Koz Got Started

"In 1974 I began a three-and-a-half year relationship with comedy legend Dick Orkin, creator of the *Chickenman* and *Tooth Fairy* radio serials, and was writer-talent on many of Orkin's radio commercials and features. With Orkin, I co-wrote sixty-five episodes of *Chickenman Returns for the Last Time Again,* which is still syndicated worldwide.

"In the late 1970s both Orkin and Jerry G. Bishop (independently) migrated to the West Coast. Before leaving, Bishop gave me permission to do *Son of Svengoolie*—an idea he had originally planned as a vehicle that he would produce with me as the next Svengoolie, which had never made it past a few false starts.

"With Bishop's blessing, I started shopping the idea around, and in June 1979, *Son of Svengoolie* premiered on Channel 32 in Chicago. It ran for six and a half years, winning three consecutive Chicago Emmy Awards for Best Entertainment Series.

"Channel 32 canceled *Son of Svengoolie* in January 1986. In the meantime I freelanced as a commercial talent-writer and was a fill-in radio host on WGN radio. Briefly, I was also weekend morning host on the Satellite Music Network's adult-contemporary format, heard all over the world.

"In 1989 I returned to Channel 32, hosting late movies both as myself and other characters. The show's premise was that I was a pirate-broadcaster breaking into the station's signal to do comedy bits. The premise was so convincing that its promos brought calls from viewers, and even the FCC, asking about the "mysterious interruptions." The show won me an additional Chicago Emmy for Best Entertainment Series.

"At the same time I was morning host on WCKG-FM, broadcasting live from such unique places as Jamaica and Disney/MGM Studios in Orlando and sharing the mike with Paul Schaeffer, Jerry 'The Beaver' Mathers, and stars of *My Three*

Sons. In 1990 I became daily host for all the Channel 32 kids' programming, later adding additional duties as weekend weatherman and host for live events, such as Taste of Chicago and New Year's Eve broadcasts.

"After leaving Channel 32 in 1993 and another round of freelancing, I joined General Manager Neal Sabin in bringing WCIU on the air at 'The U,' a mainstream, independent TV station. No longer Son of Svengoolie (his mentor, Jerry G. Bishop, having declared him 'all grown-up'), I brought the station on the air as Svengoolie!"

What the Job's Really Like

"I now portray the popular character each week on 'The U,' with his cast of Doug Graves, the laid-back, musical sidekick, and Tombstone, the talking skull. I continue to popularize rubber chickens, bad movies, and the local suburb of Berwyn. In addition to the popular musical numbers and commercial parodies Svengoolie has always been known for, each show features a segment of the movie produced in 'Svensurround,' with new sound effects, dubbed-in dialogue, and visuals. This technique was first done by Bishop and me in the 1970s, before the advent of *Mystery Science Theatre 3000.* Svengoolie's hard work and comic genius keeps paying off, 'Svengoolie—The First Year,' a look back at Svengoolie's first year on WCIU, was rewarded with a Chicago Emmy for Best Entertainment Program Special.

"I also appear on Channel 26 as myself and various other characters—whatever is needed. I am involved in many aspects of the station, both on-screen and off, and am proud to be part of one of Chicago's most creative stations, Channel 26, 'The U.'

"As far as the *Svengoolie* program goes, a typical week begins with my screening the movie for the show we're working on that week: dividing it into the proper number of segments, editing it down to time and sometimes for content, and taking notes on the film, on which to base my comedy bits in the show. During this same time, I'm working on the postproduction of the previous week's show, adding and editing production elements to make the finished program. Then I write the bits for the show, consulting with Doug Scharf, my musician crony, about what song we'll parody that week, for which he creates a complete musical track in his studio. I also work with assistants to get necessary props, costumes, and production elements we need. We then tape all the show elements—usually on Thursday. On Friday I get together all necessary elements for the postproduction that starts the next week.

"At the same time, I work on promos, specials, regular station voice-over work, and writing—and I do public appearances as Svengoolie. This TV station is unusual in that it is a smaller, family-owned station in such a major market. It is doubtful that I would get to do so much or wear so many different hats at any other station in a market this size. It is extremely hectic, with the added pressure of trying to get good ratings. I often end up working at home as well and doing extra appearances on radio and in other media. I put in well over forty hours a week, between home and the workplace. The work atmosphere is like a beehive, but very conducive to creativity. There are many people contributing in various ways to the creative process that produces the finished product, so that there is a sense of community and camaraderie. I am fortunate to work with many people, directors, and technical staff who like what we do enough to do *more* than is expected of them. I take it as a personal compliment that they want my stuff to be the best it can possibly be!

"What I like best is the satisfaction of creating good, funny stuff that keeps people entertained—quality stuff that people remember and want more of (just, as I mentioned, as it was people's fond memories that made me do the character again). I also like the fact that I have so much hands-on, creative control over what I do.

"The downside is the lack of privacy. People do recognize me, and I am aware of the possible dangers to my family from people who find out where we live. Also, the work can eat into time with my family. I find it hard to complain, though. There have been stretches with less work, and I'd rather be overworked and providing for my family than having loads of free time—and more money going out each month than is coming in!"

Expert Advice

"My advice is to have a realistic view of the business. It is *very* tough and competitive, and you really need to want to be doing this kind of stuff to survive the pressures of living and dying by ratings, the whims of management, changes in format, and so on. The key to survival is having adaptability and being able to do as many different things as possible.

"Also, don't think you can do as I did—don't send me material and think I'll hire you and you'll become 'grandson or granddaughter of Svengoolie.' I still have no problem coming up with my own material, and the Sven family line will end with me!"

INTERVIEW
Joe Hansard
Actor

Auditioning for a television commercial at the age of five was enough for Joe Hansard to become hooked, and he currently works as an actor and a stand-up comedian in New York City. He attended trade school at the Broadcasting Institute of Maryland and was an Actor-in-Residence at the International Film & Television Workshops. Other training includes Stand-Up New York (comedian school) and the Mike Fenton Scene Study Workshop for Film. He has performed his comedy routine at several comedy clubs in New York. Hansard's favorite acting credit is the part of Jimmy Lee Shields in the pilot episode of *Homicide.*

How Joe Hansard Got Started

"I've always had a fascination for the motion picture industry. I enjoy the camaraderie and collaboration that comes with a film or television project, as well as the challenges. I liken it to being in a football game, where you are given the ball and you run with it. As an actor, I try to expand on the ideas given me by bringing my own uniqueness to a role.

"I like surrounding myself with creative, enthusiastic, and energetic people. There is nothing better than working with folks who truly love their work and get excited about what they do. As a stand-up comedian, nothing is more exhilarating than laughter and applause. It is sweeter than any candy, and it doesn't rot my teeth!

"I owe everything to my mom and dad. I performed at talent showcases in elementary school, and was into magic tricks in my preteens. After high school I didn't know what I wanted to do with my life, and mom came to the rescue again by suggesting a trade school for broadcasting. I was about nineteen or twenty when I landed my first paying gig as a DJ for an AM radio station in the college town of Shippensburg, Pennsylvania.

"I got my SAG card when director Christopher Leitch cast me in a principal role in the feature film *The Hitter*, starring Ron O'Neal and Adolph Caesar (who was an Oscar winner for *A Soldier's Story*).

"I moved to Los Angeles in the early 1980s and had an absolutely horrible experience there. I couldn't get work, had my car repossessed, went bankrupt, and was in poor shape emotionally. It was the darkest time of my life, and there seemed to be no light at the end of the tunnel. But I finally got my act together and moved back east, and that's when Barry Levinson cast me in the pilot episode of *Homicide* on NBC. The 'Gone for Goode' episode, which I appear in, aired after the Superbowl in 1993 and was the highest-rated *Homicide* episode ever.

"I decided to pursue stand-up comedy as a means to network and get myself 'out there.' So far I have performed at 'Stand-Up New York,' 'The Comedy Store,' and 'The Fun Factory.'"

What the Job's Really Like

"The bulk of my typical day is actually spent looking for work. I track casting leads wherever I can find them, either through personal contacts with the industry professionals I've been associated with over the years, the Internet, or just the good old grapevine. This is a crazy business. Sometimes it's busy and full beyond belief, and there's barely time to catch my breath. At other times, weeks and even months can go by with nary a job in sight.

"If I'm working on a film or television show, the days are very long—between ten and fourteen hours. There is either a real camaraderie that forms on a set or a real paranoia, depending on any number of circumstances and variables, in or out of your control, that are inherent to the industry. In most cases, it is quite enjoyable, as cast and crew are very professional, and you more often than not will get kudos when the director or producer likes the work you are doing. I've found that the entire production and creative team literally evolves into a family.

"I like to work! I love meeting and working with creative, talented actors and directors. I love the business and wouldn't trade it for anything! But the thing I like least is not having any work—having to sit idle. I see an acting coach once a week and take classes to stay tuned up."

Expert Advice

"The most important thing is to love your work. Know that there is much competition and some lean times, but always remember to enjoy what you do and have fun doing it!"

FOR MORE INFORMATION

Information about opportunities in regional theaters may be obtained from

Theatre Communications Group, Inc.
355 Lexington Avenue
New York, NY 10017

A directory of theatrical programs may be purchased from

National Association of Schools of Theatre
11250 Roger Bacon Drive, Suite 21
Reston, VA 22090

More information on this field can be found in the following books:

- Bjorguine Bekken. *Opportunities in Performing Arts.* Lincolnwood, IL: NTC/Contemporary Publishing, 1991.

- Greenspon, Jaq. *VGM's Career Portraits—Acting.* Lincolnwood, IL: NTC/Contemporary Publishing, 1996.

- Moore, Dick. *Opportunities in Acting.* Lincolnwood, IL: NTC/Contemporary Publishing, 1998.

CHAPTER 2 Careers in Music and Dance

EDUCATION
B.A. or B.S. or formal study recommended

$$$ SALARY/EARNINGS
$5,000 and up

OVERVIEW

Musicians

Musicians include instrumentalists, singers, composers, arrangers, and conductors of instrumental or vocal performances. Musicians may perform alone or as part of a group, before live audiences or on radio, in recording studios, on television, or in movie productions.

Most musicians specialize in a particular kind of music or performance. Instrumental musicians play a musical instrument in an orchestra, band, rock group, or jazz group. Instrumentalists may play any of a wide variety of string, brass, woodwind, or percussion instruments or electronic synthesizers. Many of them learn several related instruments, such as the flute and clarinet, often improving their employment opportunities.

Singers interpret music using their knowledge of voice production, drama, melody, and harmony. They sing character parts or perform in their own individual style. Singers are often classified according to their voice range: soprano, contralto, tenor, baritone, or bass. They may also be classified by the type of music they sing, such as opera, rock, reggae, folk, rap, or country and western.

Orchestra conductors lead instrumental music groups, such as orchestras, dance bands, and various popular ensembles. Conductors audition and select musicians, choose the music to accommodate the talents and abilities of the musicians (as well as the interests of the audience), and direct rehearsals and performances, applying conducting techniques to achieve desired musical effects.

Choral directors lead choirs and glee clubs, sometimes working with a band or orchestra conductor. Directors audition and select singers and direct them at rehearsals and performances to achieve harmony, rhythm, tempo, shading, and other desired musical effects.

All musicians spend a considerable amount of time practicing, individually and in rehearsals with their band, orchestra, or other musical group. Musicians often perform at night and on weekends. Performances frequently require travel. Because many musicians find only part-time work or experience unemployment between engagements, they often supplement their income with other types of jobs. In fact, many decide they cannot support themselves as musicians and take permanent, full-time jobs in other occupations, while working only part-time as musicians.

Most instrumental musicians come into contact with a variety of other people, including their colleagues, agents, employers, sponsors, and audiences. They usually work indoors, although some may perform outdoors for parades, concerts, and dances. Certain performances create noise and vibration. In some taverns and restaurants, smoke and odors may be present, and lighting and ventilation may be inadequate.

About 256,000 musicians hold jobs. Many may be between engagements, so the total number of people employed as musicians during the course of a year might be greater. Nearly three out of five musicians who are employed work only part time; more than one of four are self-employed. Many work in cities in which entertainment and recording activities are concentrated, such as New York, Los Angeles, and Nashville. Classical musicians may perform with professional orchestras or in small chamber music groups, such as quartets or trios. Musicians may work in opera, musical comedy, and ballet productions. Many are organists who play in churches or synagogues. Two out of three musicians who are paid a salary work in religious organizations.

Musicians also perform in clubs and restaurants and for weddings and other events. Well-known musicians and groups give their own concerts, appear "live" on radio and television, make recordings and music videos, or go on concert tours. The various armed forces, too, offer careers in their bands and smaller musical groups.

Dancers

From ancient times to the present, dancers have expressed ideas, stories, rhythm, and sound with their bodies. Many perform in classical ballet. Others perform modern dance, which allows freer movement and more self-expression. Still others perform in dance adaptations for musical shows; in folk, ethnic, tap, and jazz dances; and in other popular kinds of dancing. An art form in itself, dance also complements opera, musical comedy, television, movies, music videos, and commercials. Therefore, many dancers train to sing and act, as well as dance.

Dancers most often perform as a group, although a few top artists dance solo. Many dancers combine stage work with teaching or choreography. Choreographers create original dances. They may also create new interpretations to traditional dances, such as the ballet *Nutcracker,* since few dances are written down. Choreographers instruct performers at rehearsals to achieve the desired effect. They also audition performers.

Dancing is strenuous. Rehearsals require very long hours and usually take place daily, including weekends and holidays. For shows on the road, weekend travel is common. Most performances take place in the evening, whereas rehearsals and practice generally are scheduled during the day. Dancers must also work late hours.

Due to the physical demands, most dancers stop performing by their late thirties, but they sometimes continue to work in the dance field as choreographers, dance teachers and coaches, or artistic directors. Some celebrated dancers, however, continue performing beyond the age of fifty. Professional dancers hold an average of about 24,000 jobs at any one time. Many others may be between engagements, so that the total number employed as dancers over the course of the year is hard to measure.

Dancers work in a variety of settings, including eating and drinking establishments, theatrical and television productions, dance studios and schools, dance companies and bands, and amusement parks. In addition, there are many dance instructors in secondary schools, colleges and universities, and private studios. Many teachers also perform from time to time.

New York City is home to many of the major dance companies. Other cities with full-time professional dance companies include Atlanta, Boston, Chicago, Cincinnati, Cleveland, Columbus, Dallas, Houston, Miami, Milwaukee, Philadelphia, Pittsburgh, Salt Lake City, San Francisco, Seattle, and Washington.

TRAINING

Musicians

Many people who become professional musicians begin studying an instrument at an early age. They may gain valuable experience by playing in a school or community band or orchestra, or with a group of friends. Singers usually start training when their voices mature (that is, at an older age than instrumentalists). Participation in school musicals or in a choir often provides good early training and experience. Musicians need extensive and prolonged training to acquire the necessary skill, knowledge, and ability to interpret music. This training may be obtained through private study with an accomplished musician, in a college or university music program, in a music conservatory, through practice with a group, or in some combination of these. For study in an institution, an audition usually is necessary. Formal courses include musical theory, music interpretation, composition, conducting, and instrumental and voice instruction. Composers, conductors, and arrangers need advanced training in these subjects as well.

Many colleges, universities, and music conservatories grant bachelor's or higher degrees in music. Many also grant degrees in music education to qualify graduates for a state certificate to teach music in an elementary or secondary school.

Those who perform popular music must have an understanding of, and feeling for, the style of music that interests them, but classical training can expand their employment opportunities, as well as improve their musical skills.

Although voice training is an asset for singers of popular music, many with untrained voices have successful careers. As a rule, however, young musicians take lessons with private teachers and seize every opportunity to make amateur or professional appearances.

Young people who are considering careers in music should have musical talent, versatility, creative ability, poise, and the stage presence to face large audiences.

Since quality performance requires constant study and practice, self-discipline is vital. Moreover, musicians who play concert and nightclub engagements must have physical stamina because travel and night performances are frequently required. They must also be prepared to face the anxiety of intermittent employment and rejections when auditioning for work.

Advancement for musicians generally means becoming better known and performing for greater earnings with better known bands and orchestras. Successful musicians often rely on agents or managers to find them performing engagements, negotiate contracts, and plan their careers.

Dancers

Training depends upon the type of dance. Early ballet training for women usually begins at five to eight years of age and is often given by private teachers and in independent ballet schools. Serious training traditionally begins between the ages of ten and twelve years. Men often begin their training between the ages of ten and fifteen.

Students who demonstrate strong potential in the early teens receive more intensive and advanced professional training at regional ballet schools or schools conducted under the auspices of the major ballet companies. Leading dance schools often have summer training programs from which they select candidates for admission to their regular full-time training program. Most dancers have auditioned for professional work by age seventeen or eighteen; however, training and practice never end. Professional ballet dancers have one to one-and-a-half hours of lessons every day and spend many additional hours practicing and rehearsing.

Early and intensive training also is important for the modern dancer, but modern dance generally does not require as many years of training as does ballet.

Because of the strenuous and time-consuming training, a dancer's formal academic instruction may be minimal. However, a broad, general education including music, literature, history, and the visual arts is helpful in the interpretation of dramatic episodes, ideas, and feelings.

Many colleges and universities confer bachelor's or higher degrees in dance, usually through the departments of physical education, music, theater, or fine arts. Most programs concentrate on modern dance but also offer courses in ballet or classical techniques, dance composition, dance history, dance criticism, and movement analysis.

A college education is not essential to obtaining employment as a professional dancer. In fact, ballet dancers who postpone their first audition until graduation may be at a disadvantage in competing with younger dancers. On the other hand, a college degree can help if a dancer retires at an early age, as often happens, and wishes to enter another field of work.

Completion of a college program in dance and education is essential to qualify for employment as an elementary, high school, or college dance teacher. Most colleges, as well as conservatories, require graduate degrees, but performance experience often may be substituted. A college background is not necessary, however, for teaching dance or choreographing professionally. Studio schools usually require teachers to have had experience as performers.

The dancer's life is one of rigorous practice and self-discipline; therefore, patience, perseverance, and a devotion to dance are essential. Good health and physical stamina are necessary in order to practice and perform and to follow the rugged schedule often required. Above all, one must have flexibility, agility, coordination, grace, a sense of rhythm, and a feeling for music, as well as a creative ability to express oneself through movement.

Dancers seldom perform unaccompanied, so they must be able to function as part of a team. They must be highly motivated, and should be prepared to face the anxiety of intermittent employment and rejections when auditioning for work. For dancers, advancement takes the form of a growing reputation, more frequent work, bigger and better roles, and higher pay.

JOB OUTLOOK

Musicians

Competition for music jobs is keen, and talent alone is no guarantee of success. The glamour and potentially high earnings in this occupation attract many talented individuals. However, being able to play several instruments and types of music enhances a musician's employment prospects.

Overall, employment of musicians is expected to grow faster than the average for all occupations through the year 2005. Interestingly, almost all new wage and salary jobs for musicians will arise in religious organizations and bands, orchestras, and other entertainment groups. A decline in employment is projected for salaried musicians in restaurants and bars, although they constitute a very small proportion of all salaried musicians. Bars, which regularly employ musicians, are expected to grow more slowly than eating establishments—because consumption of alcoholic beverages outside the home is expected to continue to decline. The fastest-growing segment of restaurants is the moderately priced, family-dining restaurants, which seldom provide live entertainment to their customers. Overall, most job openings for musicians will arise from the need to replace those who leave the field each year because they are unable to make a living solely as musicians.

Dancers

Dancers and choreographers face very keen competition for jobs. The number of applicants will continue to exceed the number of job openings, and only the most talented will find regular employment.

Employment of dancers and choreographers is expected to grow faster than the average for all occupations through the year 2005 due to the public's continued interest in this form of artistic expression. However, cuts in funding for the National Endowment for the Arts and related organizations could adversely affect employment in this field. Although jobs will rise each year due to increased demand, most job openings will occur as dancers and choreographers retire and leave the occupation for other reasons, and as dance companies search for and find outstanding talent.

The best job opportunities are expected to be with national dance companies because of the demand for performances outside of New York City. Opera companies will also provide some employment opportunities. Dance groups affiliated with colleges and universities, television, and motion pictures will also offer some opportunities. Moreover, the growing popularity of dance in recent years has resulted in increased employment opportunities in teaching dance.

With innovations such as electronic sounds and music videos, choreography is becoming a more challenging field of endeavor. It will continue to offer some employment opportunities for highly talented and creative individuals.

SALARIES

Musicians

Earnings depend on a performer's professional reputation, place of employment, and on the number of hours worked. The most successful musicians can earn far more than the minimum salaries indicated here.

According to the American Federation of Musicians, with classical music the minimum salaries in major orchestras range from about $1,000 to $1,200 per week during the performing season. Each orchestra works out a separate contract with its members. The season of these top orchestras range from forty-eight to fifty-two weeks, with most being fifty-two weeks. In regional orchestras, the minimum salaries are between $400 and $700 per week, and the seasons last twenty-five to thirty-eight weeks, with an average of thirty weeks. Some now work a fifty-two-week season. Community orchestras, however, have more limited levels of funding and offer salaries that are much lower for seasons of shorter duration.

Musicians employed in motion picture or television recording and those employed by recording companies are paid a minimum ranging from about $200 to $260 a week, depending on the size of the ensemble. Musicians employed by some symphony orchestras work under master wage agreements, which guarantee a season's work up to fifty-two weeks.

Many other musicians, however, may face relatively long periods of unemployment between jobs. Even when employed, however, many work part time. Thus, their earnings generally are lower than those in many other occupations. Moreover, since they may not work steadily for one employer, some performers cannot qualify for unemployment compensation, and few have either sick leave or vacations with pay. For these reasons, many musicians give private lessons or take jobs unrelated to music to supplement their earnings as performers. Many musicians belong to a local of the American Federation of Musicians. Professional singers usually belong to a branch of the Associated Actors and Artists of America.

Dancers

Earnings of many professional dancers are governed by union contracts. Dancers in the major opera ballet, classical ballet, and modern dance corps belong to the American Guild of Musical Artists, Inc., AFL-CIO; those performing on live or videotaped television belong to the American Federation of Television and Radio Artists; those who perform in films and on television belong to the Screen Actors Guild or the Screen Extras Guild; and those in musical comedies are members of the Actors' Equity Association. The unions and producers sign basic agreements specifying minimum salary rates, hours of work, benefits, and other conditions of employment. However, the individual contract that each dancer signs with the producer of the show may be more favorable than the basic agreement.

The minimum weekly salary for dancers in ballet and modern productions is about $610. According to the American Guild of Musical Artists, new first-year dancers being paid for single performances under a union agreement earn about $475 per week and $70 per rehearsal hour. Dancers on tour receive an additional per diem allowance for room and board. The minimum performance rate for dancers in theatrical motion pictures is about $100 per day of filming. The normal workweek is thirty hours, including rehearsals and matinee and evening performances, but it may be longer. Extra compensation is paid for the additional hours worked.

Earnings of choreographers vary greatly. Earnings from fees and performance royalties range from about $970 a week in small professional theaters to more than $30,000 for an eight- to ten-week rehearsal period before a Broadway production. In high-budget films, choreographers make $3,000 for a five-day week; in television, they make $7,500 to $10,000 for up to fourteen workdays.

Overall earnings from dancing are generally low because dancers' employment is irregular. Many dancers must supplement their income by taking temporary jobs unrelated to dancing.

Dancers covered by union contracts are entitled to some paid sick leave, paid vacations, and various health and pension benefits, including extended sick pay and childbirth provisions, provided by their unions. Employers contribute toward these benefits. Most other dancers do not receive any benefits.

RELATED FIELDS

There are many music- and dancing-related occupations. These include librettists, songwriters, and music therapists. A large number of music teachers work in elementary and secondary schools, music conservatories, and colleges and universities or are self-employed. Many who teach music also perform.

Technical knowledge of musical instruments is required by instrument repairers, tuners, and copyists. In addition, there are a number of occupations in the business side of music, such as booking agents, concert managers, music publishers, and music-store owners and managers, as well as salespersons of records, sheet music, and musical instruments and supplies. Others whose work involves music include disc jockeys, music critics, sound and audio technicians, music librarians, and radio and television announcers.

Career fields related to dancing include ice skaters, dance critics, dance instructors, dance notators, and dance therapists. Athletes in most sports also need the same strength, flexibility, agility, and body control as dancers.

INTERVIEW
Mark Marek
Singer and Band Owner

Mark Marek is a singer and the owner of Private Stock Variety Dance Band of Lenexa, Kansas. His background includes two years of college with course work focusing on music theory, audio and engineering, and the fundamentals of music and business.

How Mark Marek Got Started

"I started playing the drums in junior high school and then learned to play the six-string guitar. By the time I was sixteen, my brother had his own band, so I started playing and learning about bands from him. Fourteen years ago, I started my own band."

What the Job's Really Like

"My band is primarily a country club or high-dollar type band. We play mostly at weddings, country clubs, and other formal occasions. The band's working hours are usually 6:30 P.M. until 1 A.M., mostly on Fridays and Saturdays. Most gigs last three to four hours, and we have to arrive there at least an hour and a half before the start time. We generally do one-hour sets, with a twenty-minute break every hour or so. In addition to setting up, we also have to break down the equipment. Because we've been together for so long, we don't need to rehearse much, perhaps every three to four months.

"I love seeing the reaction of the audience. It's fun to know and see that they are having a good time. That's the thrill I get out of it. What I like least is the inconsistency in bookings. Each month the number of gigs changes, which affects the cash flow. The peak periods for the band are December and May to June.

"During the week, I mostly take bookings, spend time on the phone getting the specifics for each one, and contact the five band members about our schedule. I also handle all of the contracts for each performance. Aside from the band, I also give private guitar lessons and book gigs for other bands."

Expert Advice

"To approach success in the music industry, you need to have good people skills, a general sense of business, a real enjoyment of what you do, a recognition of what your niche is in the music world, patience, good customer-relations skills, expert technical skills, and a knowledge of audio and video.

"Having a band is a business, not an ego trip. You really need to have a basic knowledge of business and marketing. You can be the best musician, but in order to be successful you also have to know how to sell yourself. It's a tough way to make a living—that's why you have to have a real passion for the business."

INTERVIEW
Ed Goeke
Music Director

Ed Goeke is the music director of Christ Episcopal Church in Overland Park, Kansas. He has a B.A. and an M.A. in music education from the University of Iowa, and a master's degree from the University of Kansas in Lawrence, Kansas, where he is a Ph.D. candidate in music education.

How Ed Goeke Got Started

"I studied voice, piano, and French horn from the time I was in junior high school. Both my parents are music educators, so it was a natural thing for me to enter a career in music. Music has affected my whole life. It *is* my life. I can't imagine not having musical outlets. I will probably never leave music. What I find most gratifying is performing well, knowing that people are grateful for a job well done."

What the Job's Really Like

"Sunday is the culmination of the work I do all week. The workday starts at about 8 A.M. with warm-up for the first service, which is at 8:45 A.M. We have an ensemble of eight to ten people. When this service is over, then rehearsal starts (at 9:30 or so) for the 10:45 A.M. service. For this service, we use a choir of twenty-four people with an organist. The service is over about noon. There is a break for lunch, then about 2:30 P.M. the rehearsal starts for the 5:30 service. We organize and plan for this week's service and some for next week's selection. The day usually ends at about 7 P.M.

"It's very casual here in terms of dress and chain of command. A lot of time is spent in rehearsal and planning for worship services. The busiest time is the whole month of December due to the number of liturgies and the importance of the spiritual services.

"I took this job because it enables me to use my classical background and work in a traditional setting, but at the same time to lead others in contemporary music. I can work with a variety of musicians. It's great working with this fine group of people. I like working with a mission in mind—having a goal of bringing people closer to God through worship, providing windows of opportunity through excellent music. The music allows people to participate more actively by providing a means which inspires and moves people more deeply to develop a closer relationship with God. What I like least is reproducing [copy] music and having to stay on top of all of the paperwork.

"Church jobs are changing dramatically. The best way to be professionally equipped is to get very good at one thing. If you want to be a full-time music director of a church, then it is important to have excellent keyboard skills. I'd also recommend gaining skills in arranging and improvisational skills, and exposure to a wide variety of music. It is important to be able to work well with people. Gaining these skills can be accomplished by performing in church choirs and acquiring experience."

Expert Advice

"It's important that you are a people person, that you are a team builder and a consensus builder, that you are sensitive to people's needs, that you have a thorough knowledge of what makes music good, and that you have a background in performance. Keyboard skills, a good knowledge of literature for choirs, a background in liturgy, the ability to take available resources and arrange on the spot, good improvisational skills, the ability to communicate effectively, and good organizational skills are all pluses."

INTERVIEW
Priscilla Gale
Opera Singer

Soprano Priscilla Gale attended both the Juilliard School of Music and the Cleveland Institute of Music. She has also studied in Austria and with private teachers Luigi Ricci (in Rome) and Michael Trimble. Currently, when she's not performing with an opera company or symphony orchestra, she is a faculty member at Wesleyan University in Middletown, Connecticut, where she teaches voice.

How Priscilla Gale Got Started

"Having come from a very musical family of pianists, singers, and violinists, I was at the piano by the age of five. My family always assumed that I would pursue a career as a pianist, but I realized my real joy and fulfillment was in singing, not the piano. As I began to explore that world more thoroughly, I discovered opera and found my home. The rest is history. I received my first professional contract with the Ft. Wayne (Indiana) Symphony Orchestra during my senior year at the Cleveland Institute of Music."

What the Job's Really Like

"Every engagement you receive as a singer-performer changes you in the most wonderful way. As an artist, you grow on multiple levels, personally (inwardly and artistically), outwardly . . . and one thing leads to another. Each time, your life as an artist is changed; you grow in some immeasurable, wonderful way, and the possibilities are limitless.

"No one job site is like another. In opera the rehearsals are intense. Even with the appropriate union breaks, they are long, long days—usually over a ten- to twelve-hour period daily, and over two or perhaps three weeks. It really depends on how a company works, and they all work differently.

"Orchestra jobs for singers tend to be over a three- or four-day period. Usually you have a piano rehearsal with the conductor, then there are one or two orchestra rehearsals, followed by the performances. It is always busy and intense, but also exciting. It is fast paced, and you must know your craft. There is little room for poor preparation. And you must always have the ability to adjust to every circumstance and environment, for no two are ever the same. Each conductor is different, each director, and so on, so you must be very adaptable and professional.

"What I love most about my work is the ability to touch an audience—people whom I never meet individually, but collectively. My heart and soul meet theirs. Unfortunately, there are just not enough performance opportunities for everyone, and it is no longer possible to make a full-time living at this career unless you are one of the lucky top 20 percent."

Expert Advice

"I always tell people who want to do this kind of work to look inward and ask if there is anything else in life that will bring them happiness and fulfillment. If so, then I suggest that they do that instead. If not, then they should by all means pursue this career. But know that it is—especially in the beginning—a very difficult business and a difficult life.

"Talent is but a small piece of it. Most people cannot comprehend the level of sacrifice that this career requires. There is that wonderful, romantic notion of being the 'starving artist,' but there's nothing romantic about it when you're living it.

"With hard work, determination, perseverance, and an unwavering faith in yourself, anything can happen. The journey is an incredible ride, and one I would not have missed. And as I look back at my past, at my present, and toward my future, I can honestly say that I am one of the lucky ones."

FOR MORE INFORMATION

There are literally hundreds of professional associations for musicians. Contact any of the following for more information about employment in this field.

Academy of Country Music (ACM)
500 Sunnyside Boulevard
Woodbury, NY 11797

American Choral Directors Association (ACDA)
P.O. Box 6310
Lawton, OK 73506

American Federation of Musicians (AFM)
1501 Broadway, Suite 600
New York, NY 10036

American Federation of Television and Radio Artists (AFTRA)
260 Madison Avenue
New York, NY 10016

American Guild of Music (AGM)
5354 Washington Street
P.O. Box 3
Downers Grove, IL 60515

American Guild of Musical Artists (AGMA)
1727 Broadway
New York, NY 10019

American Guild of Organists (AGO)
475 Riverside Drive, Suite 1260
New York, NY 10115

American Music Conference (AMC)
5140 Avenida Encinas
Carlsbad, CA 92008

American Musicological Society (AMS)
201 South 34th Street
University of Pennsylvania
Philadelphia, PA 19104

American Symphony Orchestra League (ASOL)
777 Fourteenth Street, NW, Suite 500
Washington, DC 20005

Association of Canadian Orchestras
56 The Esplanade, Suite 311
Toronto, Ontario, Canada M5E IA7

Black Music Association (BMA)
1775 Broadway
New York, NY 10019

Broadcast Music, Inc. (BMI)
320 West 57th Street
New York, NY 10019

Chamber Music America
545 Eighth Avenue
New York, NY 10018

Chorus America
Association of Professional Vocal Ensembles
2111 Sansom Street
Philadelphia, PA 19103

College Music Society
202 West Spruce
Missoula, MT 59802

Concert Artists Guild (CAG)
850 Seventh Avenue, Room 1003
New York, NY 10019

Country Music Association (CMA)
P.O. Box 22299
One Music Circle South
Nashville, TN 37203

Gospel Music Association (GMA)
P.O. Box 23201
Nashville, TN 37202

International Conference of Symphony and Opera
Musicians (ICSOM)
6607 Waterman
St. Louis, MO 63130

Metropolitan Opera Association (MOA)
Lincoln Center
New York, NY 10023

National Academy of Popular Music (NAPM)
885 Second Avenue
New York, NY 10017

National Academy of Recording Arts and
Sciences (NARAS)
303 North Glen Oaks Boulevard, Suite 140
Burbank, CA 91502

National Association of Music Theaters
John F. Kennedy Center
Washington, DC 20566

National Association of Schools of Music
11250 Roger Bacon Drive, Suite 21
Reston, VA 22091

National Orchestral Association (NOA)
474 Riverside Drive, Room 455
New York, NY 10115

National Symphony Orchestra Association (NSOA)
JFK Center for the Performing Arts
Washington, DC 20566

Opera America
777 14th Street, NW, Suite 520
Washington, DC 20005

Screen Actors Guild (SAG)
7065 Hollywood Boulevard
Hollywood, CA 90028

Society of Professional Audio Recording Studios
4300 Tenth Avenue North, #2
Lake Worth, FL 33461

Touring Entertainment Industry Association (TEIA)
1203 Lake Street
Fort Worth, TX 76102

Women in Music
P.O. Box 441
Radio City Station
New York, NY 10101

For information on purchasing directories about colleges and universities that teach dance (including details on the types of courses offered) and offer scholarships, write to National Dance Association, 1900 Association Drive, Reston, VA 22091; or call 1-800-321-0789.

A directory of dance, art and design, music, and theater programs may be purchased from the National Association of Schools of Dance, 11250 Roger Bacon Drive, Suite 21, Reston, VA 22090.

For information on all aspects of dance, including job listings, send a self-addressed, stamped envelope to American Dance Guild, 31 West 21st Street, Third Floor, New York, NY 10010.

A directory of dance companies and related organizations, plus other information on professional dance, is available from Dance/USA, 777 14th Street NW, Suite 540, Washington, DC 20005.

CHAPTER **3** CHAPTER # Careers in Radio and Television

🎓 **EDUCATION**
B.A. or B.S. recommended

$$$ SALARY/EARNINGS
$22,000 and up

OVERVIEW

Announcers and newscasters are well-known to radio and television audiences. Radio announcers, often called disc jockeys, select and introduce recorded music; present news, sports, weather, and commercials; interview guests; and report on community activities and other matters of interest to their audience. If a written script is required, they may do the research and writing for it. They often ad-lib much of the commentary. They also may operate the control board, sell commercial time to advertisers, and write commercial and news copy. Some announcers at large stations specialize in sports, weather, or in general news; they may be called newscasters or anchors. Others are news analysts. In smaller stations, one announcer may do everything.

News anchors, or a pair of coanchors, present news stories and introduce in-depth videotaped news or live transmissions from on-the-scene reporters. Weathercasters, also called weather reporters or meteorologists, report and forecast weather conditions. They gather information from national satellite weather services, wire services, and other local and regional weather bureaus.

Sportscasters select, write, and deliver the sports news. This may include interviews with sports personalities and coverage

47

of games played. Sports announcers sometimes are masters of ceremonies at touchdown club banquets or are on hand to greet customers at openings of sporting goods stores.

Broadcast news analysts, called commentators, present news stories and also interpret them and discuss how they may affect the nation or listeners. Show hosts interview guests about their lives, work, or topics of current interest. Announcers also frequently participate in community activities.

Announcers and newscasters usually work in well-lit, air-conditioned, soundproof studios. The broadcast day is long for radio and TV stations. Some are on the air twenty-four hours a day, so announcers can expect to work unusual hours. Many announcers present early-morning shows, when many people are getting ready for work or commuting. Other announcers may do late-night newscasts.

These professionals work within tight schedule constraints, which can be physically and mentally stressful. For many announcers, the intangible rewards, creative work, many personal contacts, and the satisfaction of becoming widely known far outweigh the disadvantages of irregular and often unpredictable hours, work pressures, and disrupted personal lives.

Radio and television announcers and newscasters hold about fifty thousand jobs. Nearly all are staff announcers, but some are freelance announcers who sell their services for individual assignments to networks and stations or to advertising agencies and other independent producers.

TRAINING

Entry to radio and television careers is highly competitive. While formal training in broadcast journalism from a college or technical school (private broadcasting school) is valuable, station officials pay particular attention to taped auditions that show an applicant's delivery and—in television—appearance and style on commercials, news, and interviews. Those hired by television stations usually start out as production secretaries, production assistants, researchers, or reporters and are given a chance to move into announcing if they show an aptitude for on-air work. Newcomers to television broadcasting also may begin as news camera operators. A novice's chance of landing an on-air newscasting job is remote, except possibly for a small radio station. In radio, newcomers usually start out by taping interviews and operating equipment.

Many announcers begin at a station in a small community. If they are qualified, they may move to a better-paying job in a larger city. Announcers also may advance by hosting a regular program as a disc jockey, sportscaster, or other specialist. Competition for jobs is particularly intense in the national networks, and employers look for college graduates with at least several years of successful announcing experience.

Announcers must have a pleasant and well-controlled voice, good timing, excellent pronunciation, and correct English usage. Television announcers need a neat, pleasing appearance as well. Knowledge of theater, sports, music, business, politics, and other subjects likely to be covered in broadcasts improves chances for success. Announcers must also be computer literate because stories are created and edited on the computer. In addition, they should be able to ad-lib all or part of a show and to work under tight deadlines. The most successful announcers attract a large audience by combining a pleasing personality and voice with an appealing style.

High school courses in English, public speaking, drama, foreign languages, and electronics are valuable, and hobbies such as sports and music are additional assets. Students may gain valuable experience at campus radio or television facilities and at commercial stations. Some stations and cable systems offer financial assistance and on-the-job training in the form of internships, apprentice programs, co-op work programs, scholarships, or fellowships.

Before enrolling in a broadcasting school, contact personnel managers of radio and television stations, as well as broadcasting trade organizations, to determine the school's reputation for producing suitably trained candidates.

Announcers who operate transmitters must obtain a restricted radiotelephone operator permit from the Federal Communications Commission (FCC).

OUTLOOK

Competition for jobs as announcers will be very keen because the broadcasting field typically attracts many more job seekers than there are jobs. Small radio stations are more inclined to hire beginners, but the pay is low. Because competition for ratings is so intense in major metropolitan areas, large stations will continue to seek announcers and newscasters who have proved that they can attract and retain a large audience. Newscasters who are knowledgeable in such areas as business, consumer, and health news may have an advantage over others. Although specialization is more common at larger stations and the networks, many smaller stations also encourage it.

Due to the slowing in the growth of new radio and television stations and cable systems little change in the employment of announcers is expected through the year 2005. Most openings in this relatively small field will arise from the need to replace those who transfer to other kinds of work or leave the labor force. Many announcers leave the field because they cannot advance to better-paying jobs. Employment in this occupation is not significantly affected by downturns in the economy. If recessions cause advertising revenues to fall, stations tend to cut behind-the-scenes workers rather than announcers and broadcasters.

SALARIES

Salaries in broadcasting vary widely. They are higher in television than in radio, higher in larger markets than in small ones, and higher in commercial broadcasting than on public networks.

According to a survey conducted by the National Association of Broadcasters and the Broadcast Cable Financial Management Association, the average salary for radio news announcers is about $27,901. Salaries range from $23,000 in the smallest markets to $39,291 in the largest markets. Among sports announcers the average is $38,950, ranging from $26,663 in the smallest markets to $75,029 in the largest.

Among television announcers, news anchors earn an average of $65,520, their salaries ranging from $24,935 in the smallest markets to $199,741 in the largest. Weathercasters average $52,562 in salary, ranging from $25,638 to $130,919. The average salary for sportscasters is $48,704, ranging from $22,400 to $128,877.

RELATED FIELDS

The success of announcers and news broadcasters depends on how well they speak to their audiences. Oral communication skills are also vital for interpreters, sales workers, inspirational speakers, public relations specialists, teachers, and actors.

INTERVIEW
Sylvia Perez
Television News Anchor

Sylvia Perez is a WLS-TV Channel 7 anchor in Chicago. She has worked in broadcasting since 1983.

How Sylvia Perez Got Started

"I attended journalism school at the University of Oklahoma and began my journalism career in 1983. My first job was in my hometown of Lawton, Oklahoma. I did morning news cut-ins and daily reporting. In 1984 I made the decision to move to another small station in Amarillo, Texas, because the Lawton station did not have live satellite units needed to provide live capabilities.

"What an exciting time of my life this turned out to be! I received a phone call from an agent who was familiar with my demo tape (showing a sample of my work), asking if I would like to be represented by that company. The company had already successfully forwarded the tape to a station in Denver, Colorado, that was showing interest in me. With only six months' experience in Amarillo, I moved to Denver to become a morning news anchor and weekday reporter. I had worked in a small market only, and yet in a short time, I was headed to an exciting city with a medium-size market and a very professional newscast.

"After a two-year stint in Denver, I started to feel the hours beginning to take their toll. I had to arrive at 4 A.M. to write the news that I would present on the 6 A.M. show. That meant getting to bed really early so that I could get up at 2:30 A.M. and be at work on time. Needless to say, this was difficult. In addition, I didn't see the possibility of upward movement. So I decided to move on.

"Incredibly, with no forewarning, I received a call from an NBC station. The voice on the other end of the phone said, 'I've seen your tape. Would you like to be a Houston weekend anchor?' He attempted to hire me over the phone, but I flew out for an interview, and decided subsequently it would be a good career move. I spent the next two years in Houston as a medical reporter and weekend anchor. After that I decided that medical reporting was not for me. With the aid of an agent, I received a number of job offers, two of them in Chicago. My ultimate choice was WLS-TV, where I was hired as a weekday reporter and weekend anchor. Happily, in September 1992 I became the coanchor of Eyewitness News with Linda Yu (at 11:30 A.M.), the first newscast in Chicago anchored by two women."

What the Job's Really Like

"Being an anchor is really not the glamorous job everyone seems to think it is. That's because sitting behind the studio anchor desk is only a small portion of the job. A typical day means rush, rush, rush. Since I don't get off the air until noon, I get a late start on whatever my assigned story is. It might be a story that a reporter from another station is covering and had started much earlier. That means that I have to play catch-up from the start and work fast. I may only have a short time to put the story together, but I still must be thorough and make sure that I don't omit any important details. Of course, if there's some important late-breaking news, I'll be assigned to that story, which may mean going out on the street, doing interviews, gathering the facts, and then writing the story. The story is either presented live or as a self-contained piece for one of the newscasts—usually in the 5 or 6 P.M. news spot."

Expert Advice

"The reality of the job is that stations look for aggressive reporters who are not afraid to work hard. The career is demanding and extremely competitive. If you are not committed, you'll never make it. And you always have to be available—twenty-four hours a day, seven days a week. You must be eager to learn, since you are put in new situations every day that you must translate efficiently to the viewer. Sometimes you have to go on air live the minute you reach the scene of a newsworthy event, so you must really be able to think quickly on your feet.

"You need to be able to conduct effective interviews with people in all walks of life, and you must have the background and knowledge to put the story together into a cohesive and interesting form. You must be able to deal with death and destruction, which all too often are central to the news story, and still maintain your professionalism, asking the important questions with compassion and accuracy.

"Stations no longer want personalities who simply read the news. You must be able to go out on the street, get your hands dirty, and work, work, work! In this profession, you have to be flexible and ready to handle almost anything!"

INTERVIEW
Carol Stein
Radio Talk-Show Host

Carol Stein's one-hour program on WEAT radio in Florida is called *Business Opportunities with Carol Stein.*

How Carol Stein Got Started

"My background is a bit unusual in that I did not major in communications. As an undergraduate I went to the Wharton

Business School, where I majored in finance and electrical engineering. Then I went on to obtain my M.B.A. at Wharton.

"Entering the world of business, I traveled all over the globe as a consultant for several Fortune 500 companies in diverse fields. At the other end of the spectrum, I also had experience in cheerleading, modeling, aerobics, teaching, and acting. My mother is a public relations specialist and my father has a Ph.D. in chemical engineering and owns his own business, so I guess I'm a product of both worlds.

"Once you have experience, you make contacts and projects come to you. But when you are starting out, you have two options. You can either try to get hired at a television or radio station or you can approach a station with an idea for a show you wish to produce.

"At the beginning of my media career, when I was living in Washington, DC, I produced and hosted a television show. This allowed me to learn every aspect of television and gave me the opportunity to interview many high-level personalities, including President Clinton. When I moved to Florida, I took my television concept and adapted it to radio. Though I had a lack of media experience at the time, I felt confident to handle all aspects of the project. My preference was to approach it that way, so that I could become familiar with all aspects of this business: producing, being on the air, hiring talented individuals, marketing, selling, editing, and everything else. As a result, I know how to work the camera, do audio, or set up lighting. I write scripts. I know how to do graphics. I can work with a computer to perform all the digital animation."

What the Job's Really Like

"Every Saturday, I feature three business entrepreneurs, producers, entertainers, or marketing or public relations specialists—from all over the world. I find out how they got started, what problems they faced, what advice they would offer, and how success has changed their lives. My experience has been that these people are kind, down-to-earth individuals who have worked hard to earn the respect of others.

"Many people want to get into the field, but most of them are not aware that 99 percent of the effort I expend is behind the scenes. Most are intrigued by my career and say, 'Oh, you're so lucky; you meet people like Dave Thomas (founder of Wendy's), you're invited to lots of great parties, your life is so exciting.' But they don't realize that part of the reason for going to functions and parties is to promote both the show and myself and to meet new people who would be interesting to have as guests. (I've never had anyone turn me down.) Unfortunately, this makes my workweek a seven-day experience. I have to go to parties even if I'm tired. But since I love my career, I feel as if I'm not really working.

"I am involved in all aspects of the show: getting the sponsors, booking the guests, doing the research, creating interview questions, performing the interviews, and editing the tapes. So for every hour that I'm on the air, there are twenty to forty hours of preparation time that no one sees (and they are what makes the show so good). I study financial reports, perform other research at the library, visit other pertinent sites, read company literature, do anything I can to familiarize myself with the prospective guest. It is my goal to get to know my interview subjects well. Then I create new and different questions for each interview. As a result, I am often up until 2 A.M. staring at my computer, thinking I still have hours of work to complete my task. But I feel it's worth it because I can guarantee my guests that they will have a good time and be asked solid business questions."

Expert Advice

"In this business you've got to be confident about your abilities and able to take rejection. Since the commodity you are putting out there is *you*, it's hard not to take it personally when you are criticized: it feels personal. But you have to believe in yourself and what you do so passionately that you are willing to keep trying and to endure—no matter what. You must be willing to commit to the time and effort and be patient until you are able to realize your dream.

"You must also be prepared to do whatever is necessary to achieve success. For instance, my job requires that I do a lot of selling, whether it's calling up to secure a guest for a show, talking to sponsors, or promoting a newspaper article about me or the show.

"It's important to remember that as a talk-show host, the people you are interviewing are the stars, so it is your responsibility to get them comfortable enough so they can shine. Within them are the stories that people want to hear, so you need to keep your ego in check. If you are truly a good person who cares about others, people will trust you and feel comfortable with you. And if you're ethical and honest, you'll establish the right kind of reputation, which will stay with you throughout your career.

"One of the best parts of this career is that I'm excited by my work every day. I'm never bored. I meet many interesting, wonderful people, some of whom have become my friends. They encourage me and continually expand my sphere of knowledge. It's like getting my M.B.A. every day."

INTERVIEW
Brian R. Powell
Radio Personality/DJ

Brian R. Powell has been a radio personality and DJ on WCIL-FM radio in Carbondale, Illinois, for the past two years. His show is featured from 3 in the afternoon until 7 P.M.

How Brian R. Powell Got Started

"As a sophomore in high school I was flunking English. My teacher took me aside and said, 'You know Brian, you are articulate and have a nice voice. You should try out for the high school radio station.' I had no idea that such a thing existed, but I decided to check into it. Before I knew it, I had completed an audition and was doing a five-minute sportscast every day. It soon dawned on me that I could joyfully pursue this as a career (though I didn't know how to go about it at that point).

"I worked in high school radio for three years and gained substantial experience in proper breathing techniques, how to present myself, technical aspects of the business, and other performance and behind-the-scenes endeavors, such as writing and editing.

"When I was a senior in high school I had an electronics teacher who was also chief engineer for WBBX, a suburban radio station in Highland Park, Illinois. He was able to get me a part-time job at the station for a whopping $2.30 an hour. After a stint in radio sales, I enrolled at Southern Illinois University, where I secured a job at SIU's radio station, WSRJ. The classes that I took in radio and television were helpful, and my hours at the radio station provided a wealth of information. I settled in and enjoyed my radio years there.

"Following this, I got a part-time position at WHBI in Heron, where I worked my way up to the prestigious morning position. There I increased my knowledge and gained experience in doing play-by-play (the most difficult job in broadcasting). After about three years, I secured the morning position at VVTAO in Murphysboro, just ten miles away.

"Circumstances pushed me out of the radio business for a few years, until I moved back to Carbondale in 1992 and found my way to WCIL-FM. When I first came to the station, I was assigned the overnight shift from 2 A.M. until 6 A.M. Then I volunteered to take the 10 A.M. to 2 P.M. slot for a vacationing DJ (and for a while I did both shifts). As a result, I impressed the general manager and won the afternoon spot. I'm happy with this time slot, because I get to sleep as late as I wish, whereas morning DJs must wake up at 4:30 or 5 A.M. Another bonus of this job is that I don't have to get dressed up; I frequently arrive at the station in sweatpants, a T-shirt, and open-toed sandals. Most of the time I'm not seen by anybody, unless we have a radio tour on the calendar.

"I enjoy meeting the touring elementary and high school students. Often they have a preconceived notion of how complicated a radio station must be, and I have the opportunity to teach them about how simple it all is. The one negative aspect to these occasions is that I don't get to enjoy the privacy I usually have. When I'm alone in the radio room, I feel I have the freedom to take chances, let my mind go, and be creative, with no one staring at me. I want to be known—but not well-known. Television is a totally different medium. Those involved in it understand that since their physical image is familiar, they can't go out in public without being recognized and possibly approached. In radio, my friends know who I am, but I don't have any pretenses about being famous.

"My ultimate goal is to do radio in Chicago, although I'd consider moving to Milwaukee or St. Louis. The longer I'm involved in radio, the more I realize I still have a way to go in perfecting my craft. But I'm very willing to put in the time and energy to accomplish this because I really enjoy what I'm doing."

What the Job's Really Like

"For me, this job is really quite informal and simple. I come in about an hour early and read as much of the newspapers as possible: the *Chicago Tribune, St. Louis Post Dispatch, Southern Illinois,* and a couple of smaller local papers. I look through them to familiarize myself with what is newsworthy locally, regionally, and nationally. This is important, because I frequently receive phone calls when we're on the air from people wanting information about things that are going on in the world.

"We also receive trade publications published by record companies, which provide a wealth of information about music and the bands that we're playing. So I'll look through those as well.

"When it's actually time to go on the air, I go into the studio to select the music to play. Since we're a top-40 station, most of the music that we present repeats itself regularly about every four or five hours. The newest music is played most often. But since I'm also able to play selections of my own choice from the music that's provided in the library, I'll browse there to find songs I haven't played recently or something that looks interesting. Once I've made my selections, I organize the order of the songs so that the music is presented in a pleasing sequence and avoids abrupt changes.

"Usually the DJ who's on before me will pull the commercials that I need for the first hour of the show. So when I arrive each day, a stack of them is on the cart ready for me. Most of the commercials are prerecorded, but I do have some 'live reads,' which are fun because I can really ham them up. And I have responsibility for organizing the commercials into what we call 'top sets' or groupings, to make sure competitors are not played back-to-back (for instance, playing an ad for Coca Cola and then one for Pepsi).

"On occasion I conduct brief interviews. I'm always free to proceed with such projects if I feel they would make 'good radio.' For instance, we recently had an interesting situation involving George Harrison's sister, who used to live in a house in southern Illinois. Back in 1963, before the Beatles ever came to America, George Harrison visited and stayed with her in that home. Not only that, he played a few songs on guitar in one of the local restaurants in town. Subsequently, this house was sold to the Illinois Department of Mines and Minerals who wanted to tear it down. This became a controversy, with people taking one side or the other. Since there was considerable local interest in this issue, I did a number of live interviews with some of the people involved, including Louise Harrison herself. In the end, the house was preserved.

"Much of what comes out of my mouth is not pre-scripted. What I say is whatever feels right to say at the time. In general, I try to minimize my speaking and emphasize the music, since I feel most people are listening at work or in their cars and have a desire to hear music—not talking."

Expert Advice

"If you are interested in a radio career, the first thing you should do is make the radio a priority: listen to the DJs, what they say, and how they say it. Also be aware of what they don't say. When I was starting out, I would try to repeat exactly what the DJ was saying right after it came out of his mouth, using the very same pacing and inflection. Try doing this mimicry—or any kind of performing for that matter—in front of an audience.

"In terms of classes, focus on English. It worked for me. I had B-pluses by the time I graduated. Also concentrate on journalism, psychology, and (my personal favorite) political science. They complement radio work by sharpening your mind, thus allowing you to process information and think more quickly on your feet. These qualities are vital to success in radio.

"Perhaps the most important advice I could offer is to be prepared for failure, because if you are prepared for that, you will definitely be prepared for success."

INTERVIEW
Chuck Woodford
Radio Show Host

Chuck Woodford is the Morning Show host on KXPK (The Peak) Radio in Denver. He received a B.A. in broadcast journalism from West Virginia University, working in the college radio station for three years in various capacities, including production director and as operations manager. He heartily recommends the college radio environment, which he feels taught him "volumes."

How Chuck Woodford Got Started

"While I was growing up, my mom got me hooked on old-time radio shows like *The Shadow* and *X-1.* When I got to college, I met several folks who shared the passion that I had for the medium. As I've grown older, I've become much more educated to the ways of the business side of the industry, but I still have a great passion for the 'Theatre of the Mind' aspect of the job."

What the Job's Really Like

"Doing a show in the morning is a completely different thing than at just about any other time of the day. People rely on you to be a news provider, a sportscaster, a competent weatherman, a traffic reporter, and an entertainer. You need to be up on current events and have a passion for what you do.

"My day starts at about 4:30 A.M. when I get into work. I'm lucky in that I have a morning show producer who gets in before I do and spends about thirty minutes on the Internet, hunting down entertainment news. After I get there, we have a fifteen-minute meeting about what the focus of the show should be: Did anything interesting happen overnight? Do we have something cool to give away? Are there any shows we should be talking about (both upcoming concerts and TV shows from last night)? The show runs from 5:30 A.M. to 10 A.M. Following that, we sit down with our program director and figure out what's up for tomorrow's show. I'm usually out of the building by 1 P.M., but then it's off to do a promotion or to go host a preshow party before a big concert.

"One thing that surprised me initially about the morning slot is the amount of preparation that goes into the show. It's very time-consuming, but when you're able to pull off a great bit the next day, you know that it was all worth it.

"What I like most about my job is that it's a great avenue for my personality. I get to be myself on the radio, I have the freedom to pursue my own ideas about what the show should be, and I get to use the creativity of a talented staff around me. Plus, I don't have to wear any shoes while I'm at work, which is nice!

"I have a very difficult time, however, dealing with the corporate aspect of this industry. So few owners have spent so much money on purchasing these stations that they feel they can't take many risks. In that respect, I think the radio industry is suffering, and I find that very frustrating."

Expert Advice

"Be prepared to work as hard as you can possibly imagine. Don't expect things to fall into your lap. Don't feel you can get a really sweet gig and then coast right through it. There will always be somebody behind you willing to do the exact same job that you're doing—only with more energy and more excitement. So always push yourself."

INTERVIEW
Robin Truesdale
Television News/Video Editor

Robin Truesdale earned a Bachelor of Science degree in journalism from the University of Colorado, with an emphasis in broadcast management. She worked at Denver television station KUSA-TV for ten years as a videotape editor. She has also done freelance work for FOX News in Denver and WXIA-TV in Atlanta. Throughout her career, she has attended seminars and classes specific to video-editing techniques and new technology.

How Robin Truesdale Got Started

"I was attracted to editing after watching my dad work in the advertising field. He was a producer and director when I was a child. Sometimes I went with him on shoots and edit sessions, and got to watch the editor and him create advertising spots. It was fascinating to me to watch the editor sit at an enormous board full of buttons and switches and make 'magic' happen on video, combining music, pictures, and effects. I loved the creativity involved and the respect that the editors had. My dad had favorites to work with, whom he felt were the most talented in the Atlanta area. I regarded those top-notch video editors as being in the same league with film editors. Some had national reputations. And when I would see a national advertising spot that my dad had produced, I felt a sense of pride. I guess I wanted to feel that pride for myself as an editor.

"My internship at KUSA in my senior year of college was vital in my getting a job upon graduation. I was familiar with that specific newsroom and its expectations for news editors. It allowed me to demonstrate my abilities to the staff. Experience is really the only way to learn how to edit. The internship, combined with my experiences with my father, helped me to understand the basic concepts of editing, and that understanding made me a good candidate when a job became available."

What the Job's Really Like

"The typical day for a television news editor involves a lot of downtime and then sudden bursts of activity. There are relaxed hours in the day when editors are waiting for scripts to be written, video to be shot, and so forth. Paperwork is done during this time, dubs are made, people joke around a lot, and the mood is very light. As news time gets closer, though, the mood becomes more serious, often intense; everyone switches gears. Editors are expected to do their jobs in a short amount of time, and there is a lot of deadline pressure. As soon as scripts start coming in, work must be done quickly, but also correctly and with style. Crews often feed video from the field, and it is the editor who receives this video and turns it around, sometimes within a matter of seconds, to get it on the air. The image of people running down halls with videotape in hand is accurate. We occasionally have crashes in the hallway when people are rushing around during a newscast. So that element of the job is stressful and high pressure. It can also be exhilarating, and, in fact, that is what some people like most about the job. There is a terrific sense of satisfaction after a show is over and all has gone well.

"On the other hand, there is a lot of reprimanding when an element of the show crashes and burns. Each person has to take responsibility for the job—the results of their work are broadcast to thousands or even millions of people. The consequences of doing a poor job are pretty severe.

"Editors in news usually work a forty-hour shift, with overtime a necessity during breaking news. An editor is generally on call at all times if something big happens, like an airplane crash or large-scale emergency. You're expected to care enough about the station you work for to be there in a crisis situation, even if you are not called in right away. It's really just part of the job.

"I love the camaraderie of the news business. The atmosphere of delivering news, both good and bad, is probably somewhat like working in an emergency room. There are tragic moments, and there are triumphant ones, too. It creates a strong bond among employees . . . almost a family atmosphere. That is the part I like the most, the closeness among us all.

"On a personal level, there is a great sense of satisfaction in having done a job well. At times the editor is allowed a great deal of creativity, in cutting feature stories for instance, and that is when I have the most fun as an editor. Some pieces can really impact viewers; that makes me feel good and also important. Taking elements of a story—pictures, interviews, sound, and sometimes music—and blending them together to tell a story is a very personal thing. It requires skill and talent, and with editing you are rewarded every day by your own creations.

"The worst part of editing news is the tragic stories you come face-to-face with daily. You're exposed regularly to the worst side of humanity, the most tragic and sad events. I've edited many stories with tears streaming down my face. Those are the hard times, and the ones that really challenge you. At those times, I wish I was in commercial production or some other aspect of editing in which you have more control over your material. But there are enough positives to balance out those times."

Expert Advice

"My advice to those interested in editing of any kind is to get internships! Get as many as you can while in school, even if they're not exactly the field you're interested in. Any experience in television or film, even in still photography or writing, will enhance your education and perhaps even change your mind about what you want to do. Hands-on experience is necessary.

"Be humble. Listen to others with experience in the field. Never think you know it all, because surely you don't. Every person you meet, every experience you have, even the negative ones, will teach you something, so you must be open to learning.

"Editing is a creative, artistic field. It is also technical, being digital- and computer-based. Learning to operate equipment is critical, but a student of editing needs to do more than simply push buttons and put pictures together. It's a career that combines photography, technical skill, quick judgment, and artistic vision.

"Most of all, have confidence in yourself and don't give up. You can accomplish anything if you want it badly enough."

FOR MORE INFORMATION

For a list of schools that offer programs and courses in broadcasting, contact

Broadcast Education Association
1771 N Street NW
Washington, DC 20036

For information on FCC licenses, write to

> Federal Communications Commission
> Consumer Assistance Office
> 1270 Fairfield Road
> Gettysburg, PA 17325-7245
> or call toll free 1-800-322-1117

General information on the broadcasting industry is available from

> National Association of Broadcasters
> 1771 N Street NW
> Washington, DC 20036

For information on careers in broadcast news, contact

> Radio-Television News Directors Association
> 1717 K Street NW, Suite 615
> Washington, DC 20006

CHAPTER 4 Careers Behind the Scenes in Music and Acting

EDUCATION
B.A./B.S. or formal training recommended

$$$ SALARY/EARNINGS
$15,000 to $45,000 and up

OVERVIEW

Music

When you were younger and taking part in performances, did you long to be the center of attention with all eyes focused on you or did you prefer staying in the background and helping with props, lighting, or sound? When you went to a performance, did you ever think about what was going on behind the scenes? Did you ever consider how many people had a role in making sure that everything went according to plan?

Most people have little if any idea of what goes on behind the scenes and how many professionals perform a variety of tasks to make a performance successful and as entertaining as possible. Team spirit is of the utmost importance for the professionals who work together behind the scenes to create performances that everyone can be proud of. Those who work behind the scenes include stage managers, sound engineers, boom operators, sound-production mixers, sound and lighting technicians, music video producers, and record producers.

Behind-the-scenes technicians may find employment with a local or well-known regional band. The best strategy is to start small and try to work your way to larger and better-known bands. Major tours usually traverse Los Angeles, New York

City, and Nashville, although they may be found in almost any substantial-size city in the United States.

STAGE MANAGERS Stage managers are in charge of everything involved in onstage performances, whether they are held at clubs, concert halls, state fairs, theaters, or wherever. All aspects of a performance come under the stage manager's domain—curtain changes, lighting, sound—anything and everything that might affect the success of the performance. He or she is thus in charge of all technicians, assistants, and helpers: the entire staff.

Important stars sometimes travel with their own crews of lighting and sound technicians. The stars feel more at ease knowing that their own crews are familiar with what needs to be done and there will be no unpleasant "surprises" before, during, or after performances.

SOUND TECHNICIANS/SOUND ENGINEERS Sound technicians are important members of the behind-the-scenes staff. Answering to the tour coordinator, they usually arrive at the performance location in advance of the performers. Along with the rest of the crew, sound technicians unload and set up the equipment and the instruments. All of the equipment must be positioned so that the instruments will sound best and the vocals, if part of the performance, will blend in a pleasing manner.

Once things are set up, the vocalists and musicians arrive, and the sound technicians prepare for a very important event: the sound check. This is accomplished by having each person play his or her instrument or sing, while technicians judge whether the sound is coming through properly. Obviously, any changes that need to be made will be taken care of before the show begins.

While the show is in progress, sound technicians are in charge of the sound board, usually situated in front of the stage. In this position, they can adjust the volumes of voices and instruments.

After the show, sound technicians usually pack up the sound equipment. In some cases, they may be responsible for checking all of the equipment to see what is not working properly or is in need of repair. Sometimes sound technicians are capable of actually taking care of the problem.

BOOM OPERATORS The boom is a large overhead microphone that hangs over the set. This technician makes sure that the boom is properly following the performers.

SOUND-PRODUCTION MIXERS The sound-production mixer is in charge of the overall sound quality and the volume of the sound. Required when there is more than one microphone on the set, sound-production mixers make sure that sound is picked up and blended in a harmonious way.

MUSIC VIDEO PRODUCERS Music video producers are in charge of everything relating to the making of music videos. This operation includes all the visual effects and interpretations of the songs that vocal artists are endeavoring to convey. Producers oversee the entire production team, including the film editor, choreographer, photography director, and other team members.

Music video producers must be superb problem solvers and have good visual and listening proficiencies, the ability to work well with others, a good business sense, a sufficient understanding of the video business, and good contacts in the industry.

RECORD PRODUCERS Many people take part in the process of record production, perhaps the most important among them being the record producer. This individual has the important responsibilities of handling all payroll tasks, supervising the recording sessions, helping to decide what songs will be recorded, and actually producing the records for the artists. Other responsibilities include finding a suitable recording studio, arranging the recording time, choosing an engineer, picking an arranger, and getting in touch with a contractor—someone who can find the background musicians and vocalists needed. Record producers will also act as the heads of the operations, making sure everyone meets their responsibilities. While actually recording, the producer works hand in hand with the engineer to create the exact sound desired.

RECORDING ENGINEERS The recording engineer operates the sound board and other electrical equipment when recordings are made.

RECORDISTS This technician operates the tape machine and makes sure that everything is recorded properly.

RERECORDING MIXERS Rerecording mixers complete sound tracks by adding background music, additional dialogue, or sound effects.

Acting

Those who work with actors behind the scenes include stage directors, stage managers, technical directors, set designers, costume designers, hair stylists, makeup artists, lighting designers, sound designers, property designers, carpenters, scenic artists, wardrobe supervisors, special effects specialists, riggers, and broadcast technicians.

All the opportunities open to actors and actresses are also available to those who work behind the scenes. These would include Broadway productions, regional plays, children's theater, summer stock, radio, television, and commercials.

STAGE DIRECTORS At the top of the backstage hierarchy are stage directors who read each play to decide whether they are interested in directing it. If a stage director decides to take on the project, he or she coordinates the entire production of the play. Meetings then take place between director and playwright to decide about the best way to present it. Additional conversations will take place with the producer about such issues as casting, budgets, production schedules, and designers.

Directors are the people who interpret the plays or scripts as they see fit. In addition, they may audition and select cast members, conduct rehearsals, and direct the work of the cast and crew. Directors use their knowledge of acting, voice, and movement to achieve the best possible performance; they also usually approve the scenery, costumes, choreography, and music.

Once directors have become familiar enough with the play to determine the approach and perspective they wish to take, they meet with designers to begin the process of creating costumes, scenery, sound effects, and lighting. With the aid of a stage manager, directors make hundreds of decisions in order to best represent the piece.

Once rehearsals begin, directors are the ones who instruct the cast about where they are to be positioned on stage, how they are to move, and what feelings and actions they should display. A director rehearses the performers as they practice their lines, making suggestions for changes as appropriate.

Directors often like to attend a dress rehearsal or preview and position themselves in different parts of the theater to observe the reactions of people in the audience. Even at that point, changes can be made if the director feels they would improve the play.

Directors and producers often work under stress as they try to meet schedules, stay within budgets, and resolve personnel problems in putting together a production.

STAGE MANAGERS Once the director leaves the production, a stage manager has the final say on most everything to do with the play and its production. Stage managers are the ones who call the casts together to begin rehearsals. They see to it that everyone is present whenever their presence is required. They send an assistant to inform the stars when they will be needed and when to be ready to go onstage. If necessary, they make arrangements for stand-ins. They are the ones who signal for the house lights to dim, alerting everyone to the fact that the production is about to begin.

The stage manager maintains a master script or a book containing all details of the play. Listed inside is every actor's movements, entrance and exit cues, costume details, and lighting and sound cues. Any changes are recorded in the master book. The stage manager also maintains personnel records on all cast members and backstage workers, including their names, addresses, and phone numbers.

Assistants may help a stage manager with the backstage duties. If so, the manager can be out front to watch the play and stay attuned to changes or improvements that can be made.

TECHNICAL DIRECTORS Technical directors are assigned the task of coordinating the work of designers and their entire crews. They are responsible for making sure that all of the preliminary work moves forward on schedule and that everything fits together properly. They meet with lighting, property, and sound designers together to work out details. Also, they make sure set changes and storage details work as planned. When a production is on tour, technical directors help other workers make adjustments to fit the space and layouts of different theaters.

SET DESIGNERS Set designers are entrusted with the responsibility of the physical environment of the play. To successfully create the environment they research the time   and place of the play. Uncovering typical architecture for the time and place, a set designer makes sketches and models of possible sets and presents them to the director for his or her approval. Then the designer makes detailed drawings and models (exactly to scale) using cardboard, wood, plastic, clay, or other materials. The plans must show ways to prepare and move the pieces quickly and safely and how remaining sets may be stored offstage while one is being used onstage.

Set designers may meet with directors concerning details of construction costs and other relevant issues. On the other hand, they may take their plans to two or three shops for bids. The designers then oversee the building and painting of the sets, whether this means creating stairs, mountains, balconies, or whatever else might be needed for the play.

COSTUME DESIGNERS Costume designers must also do some researching about the locale, period, and social background of the play. Libraries and museums are appropriate places to study clothing, styles, and fabrics. When this stage is completed, they begin to draw sketches of costumes, which will eventually need the director's approval. Once given, they bring the sketches to the theater costume shop to plan how to make them. If the production is taking place in a large city, such as New York, costume designers may secure bids from two or three costume shops. They select the fabric, approve the clothing patterns, and stay abreast of how the costumes are developing. For plays that will take place with a modern setting, costume designers might also shop for ready-made garments. Other pieces, such as wigs or beards, may be needed, and the costume designer will select them from a wig shop.

Once everything is secured, fittings are scheduled for cast members to make sure everything is right. To make sure everything looks the way it should, a dress parade is then held onstage under stage lights with scenery and props in place.

HAIRSTYLISTS AND MAKEUP ARTISTS Hairstylists and makeup artists use cosmetics, pencils, greasepaints, brushes and other materials to make the actors and actresses look like the characters they play. Makeup may also include hair, clay, or plastics to create wrinkles, warts, bald heads, teeth changes, burns, or scars. Even an actor's and actress's hands must be right for the character they are playing.

LIGHTING DESIGNERS Lighting designers use lighting fixtures, patterns, color filters, and dimmers to create lighting effects. Referring to floor plans of the sets, they decide where to place each piece of equipment. The master electrician and lighting director plan the electric circuits for the equipment. The lighting-board operator controls the lights in the theater throughout the play. Cue sheets will allow the operator to know exactly when to turn each unit on and off. In some cases, a computer in the light board handles these details, which expands the effects of lighting designs. In order to make sure that circuits and lights are in proper working order, lighting designers report for work one hour before rehearsals or performances.

SOUND DESIGNERS Sound designers are the individuals who create and direct the making of sound effects: drumbeats, sirens, breaking glass, whirling tornadoes. The designers are faced with choosing and directing the placement of amplifiers, speakers, synthesizers, microphones, and other equipment. Once they are satisfied with the results, they make up cue sheets for the sound-board operator to follow during all performances. One or more sound technicians work during a show. One may work from a place in the audience, mixing or blending the sounds the audience hears. Another, backstage, may control sounds the performers and musicians hear. A third worker may be in charge of handling prerecorded sounds or special sound effects. All wear intercom headsets to monitor the work going on.

PROPERTY DESIGNERS Property designers are involved in planning and, in some cases, directing the making of pieces needed for productions—anything from palm trees to antique sofas. They may be asked to provide books, violins, spears, shields, or a wide variety of other items. They may also be asked to construct masks or even hands for characters appearing as dragons, monkeys, monsters, donkeys, or any other animal.

CARPENTERS AND SCENIC ARTISTS Working with such materials as wood, canvas, muslin, metal, and clay, carpenters and scenic artists build the sets and properties for a theatrical production.

SPECIAL-EFFECTS SPECIALISTS Special-effects specialists are the people who create, plan, and install the devices needed to make smoke, rain, snow, fog, or the like.

ELECTRICIANS Electricians connect and mark the circuits for both sound and lighting effects.

RIGGERS Riggers do their work considerably above ground level—hanging lighting, sound equipment, and scenery from wires and ropes. They also work with pulleys and counterbalances to control the movable parts of any sets.

BROADCAST TECHNICIANS Broadcast technicians operate and maintain the equipment used to record and transmit radio and television programs. They work with sound and video recorders, television cameras, transmitters, microphones, and equipment used for special effects.

WARDROBE SUPERVISORS Once the play opens, wardrobe supervisors are in charge of all of the costumes. Crews are hired to keep the shoes polished, suits brushed, broken zippers replaced, and hems stitched. Costumes may also need to be adjusted to fit stand-ins. When a production is on tour, the wardrobe supervisors and their helpers are charged with packing and unpacking the costumes and putting them in the dressing rooms.

TRAINING

Music

Although a formal education is not required for working behind the scenes in music, it can provide you with a concrete background of information and contacts. Many people interested in the music production field acquire basic knowledge and experience by "shadowing" individuals who are already performing this kind of work. Working as a volunteer in community, church, or school productions offers valuable experience, which will help improve your marketability in the music business.

It's important for behind-the-scenes personnel to be able to work well with all kinds of people. These staff members are a link in the chain that provides the totality of music performances. Other desirable characteristics include reliability and a sense of responsibility; a good ear for music; sufficient musical and technical knowledge; proficiency with the sound board, sound equipment, and electronics; and, of course, a love of music.

Acting

Many schools at the high school (and sometimes the middle school) level have programs in fine arts. Students who plan to work in theater should take part in school plays and musical shows. In high school they should also take history, literature, art, and English.

Hopefuls for careers behind the scenes should get as much experience as possible working on productions in school, church, or local theater. An association with a professional company is an added bonus. Working as a volunteer is also a good idea. Part-time possibilities include local theater, dinner theater, and special events, such as benefits or rock concerts.

Candidates for these careers should plan on earning at least a bachelor's degree in fine arts with a major in drama. Those who plan to focus on lighting and sound design may take courses in design, electricity, art, history, computers, electronics, mathematics, physics, and sound. Set designers may decide to place their major in architecture. They should take drawing, art and art history, drafting, and sculpture. Makeup artists must know something about anatomy. And they should also take sculpture, portrait painting, and other art topics. Most directors, stage managers, and designers earn a Master of Arts or Master of Fine Arts in drama or another specialty.

On a more personal level, it is important that directors and designers have a strong artistic sense, along with the ability to make decisions and instill confidence in others. Managers who are organized, possess strong leadership skills, and can inspire teamwork, are bound for success. Stage production workers need to be enthusiastic, energetic, confident, creative, and intelligent. They also need to have a good sense of humor and the ability to handle both successes and failures.

JOB OUTLOOK

Music

Since the competition for jobs is so fierce for those behind the scenes in music, even seasoned workers have long periods between jobs. Although stage workers do have more steady employment than actors or dancers, many spend weeks and months at other jobs.

There are possibilities for individuals to become record producers but only after they have paid their dues and amassed knowledge and built reputations. Once this happens, producers can go to other, more prestigious labels that pay higher salaries.

Acting

Competition is very stiff for behind-the-scenes professionals. Many technicians are first hired as *grips* (individuals who move equipment such as cameras, etc.) and then work their way up. The emergence of cable television has produced a need for more technicians.

It is an advantage if you can fill more than one slot—such as designing both sets and props or making and remodeling costumes as well as designing them. Your chances of getting work are greater having multiple skills.

SALARIES
Music

Sound technicians who work for a local band that is just getting started may earn only minimum wage or even less. As an average, however, sound technicians earn about $15,000 to about $45,000 or more each year. Higher salaries go to sound technicians who accompany better-known groups on the road. (It is also important to consider that if the sound technician is a freelancer, he or she may not work every week.)

Earnings and benefits vary widely, depending on the location, medium, and experience of the individual. The following represent typical averages:

Broadcast technicians, radio—$440 per week

Broadcast technicians, television—$500 per week

Sound-crew members—$500 to $600 per week for eight performances (New York)

Beginning sound mixers—$700 to $800 per week

Mixers with experience—$1,400 per week

Sound recordists—$840 per week

Stage managers—$12,000 to $40,000 and up, annually

Music-video producers (annually)

- Entry-level trainees—$16,000 to $18,000

- Experienced music-video producers—
  $35,000 to $40,000

- Producer with his or her own company—
  $100,000 to $300,000

Staff record producers may be entitled to a salary plus royalties on the numbers of records produced. This may amount to $18,000 to $45,000 annually and up. Those who freelance will probably be paid a fee by the artist or the record label, in addition to royalties on works produced. Terms will vary considerably, depending on who you are and what your established reputation is. It is possible for a record producer to earn in excess of $250,000 per year.

Acting

Earnings of stage directors vary greatly. According to the Society of Stage Directors and Choreographers, summer theaters offer compensation including royalties (based on the number of performances) usually ranging from $2,000 to $8,000 for a three- to four-week run of a production. Directing a production at a dinner theater will usually pay less than a summer theater but has more potential for royalties. Regional theaters may hire directors for longer periods of time, increasing compensation accordingly. The highest-paid directors work on Broadway productions, typically earning $80,000 annually, plus royalties.

The following figures represent sample rates for summer theater jobs:

Stage directors—$500 to $2,500 a show

Stage managers—$150 to $350 per week

Costume designers—$500 to $1,500 a show

Set designers—$350 to $1,000 or more for each design

Lighting and sound designers—$110 to $330 or more per week

Property coordinators—$110 to $200 or more per week

Technical directors—$110 to $220 or more per week

Painters, carpenters, electricians—$110 to $330 or more per week

Wardrobe workers—$100 to $150 or more per week

Nearly all stage production workers belong to a union, some to more than one federation. In New York City the Broadway and off-Broadway workers must belong to a union. In other locations the requirements vary. Actors' Equity Association is a large, strong union to which actors and stage managers belong. Some theaters will only employ Equity actors or Equity stage managers.

Behind-the-scenes workers may be paid by the week, month, or season.

Those who are truly skilled at what they do often get much more than a minimum amount. For example, though most riggers earn about $15 per hour, one who is experienced might get $3,000 for a single rock concert.

Some summer theaters offer internships with a modest stipend. Some summer programs offer $500 to $900 for the season to assistant designers, stage managers, and technical directors. Technical production interns and shop assistants may be offered $75 per week.

Salaries for beginner broadcast technicians at radio and television stations range from $190 to $330 per week. Experienced technicians earn $330 to $1,000 per week. Union technicians are entitled to union scale.

RELATED FIELDS

Careers related to working behind the scenes in music include roadie, audio technician, sound engineer, lighting technician, assistant stage manager, engineer-producer, recording engineer, recording assistant, recording studio clerk, engineer, grip, and stagehand.

Occupations related to acting include communications technicians, drama teachers, motion picture directors, script supervisors, program assistants (radio and television), announcers, disc jockeys, and narrators. Other roles are film editors, communications technicians, miniature-set constructors, recordists, sound cutters, microphone boom operators, dubbing machine operators, and film loaders.

Still more possible options include drama teachers, actors and actresses, dramatic coaches, fashion designers, furniture designers, interior designers, artists' managers, booking managers, circus agents, location managers, and real estate appraisers.

INTERVIEW
Ross Norton
Stage Manager, Lighting Systems Technician

Ross Norton's educational background includes an associate's degree in instructional technology from the University of Phoenix. His work experience comprises positions as production/stage manager, backline/guitar technician, and lighting systems technician in Nashville, Tennessee.

How Ross Norton Got Started

"I always wanted to be close to the music. As a teenager I was a regular concertgoer and found myself always wanting more. I felt that making a living working around something that gave me so much pleasure was the best of both worlds.

"Over the years I have acquired quite a few different job descriptions as the need arose. I originally started out with a lighting company that leased out lights and crews to go with them to different bands touring the circuit of major venues. I now do stage managing and production, and was recently the site coordinator for Country Fest '96 in Atlanta."

What the Job's Really Like

"Lighting presents a kind of work that is definitely the most brutal. The gear is awkward and heavy. The work hours are long, thankless, and dirty, and the pay for a beginner is next to nothing. Lights are always the first in and the last out, and you will earn every nickel of spare time that you can find. There is no glamour, and never has been, to this lifestyle. Lighting technicians are definitely the hardest working and most durable of all touring personnel.

"It does, however, provide you with a foot in the door to an otherwise-closed room. It will allow you to get a glimpse of how things work at a show to help you decide if you want to work in this industry or not.

"It won't seem so at first, but all shows are basically run the same way. A typical day starts weeks in advance, with calls from the band's production manager to the local promoter who is sponsoring the show. This is called advance work, and how well it's done can definitely affect your day. This is where the number of stage hands (local boys and girls brought in to help the road crew) is decided, and all the stage and rigging require-ments are hashed out so there will be as few surprises as pos-sible when the trucks arrive. Each lighting and sound configuration is different with each band. Every single cable, chain, and bulb is brought in by the band unless otherwise ordered (and when we leave, nothing is left but dust and an empty stage).

"The trucks usually arrive about eight or nine in the morn-ing, and since you are paying for the local crew whether you use them or not, you had best be quick. The riggers will climb up into the ceiling of the venue and begin hanging points. These are motors that hoist up the lights and sound above the stage. The lighting crew will begin assembling the lighting rig on the stage. A good stage manager will already have checked out the condition of the stage to make sure that it is level, big enough (as per your advance work), and has no weak spots that could cave as gear is added to it. While the lights are being assembled on stage, the sound PA is being unloaded and pushed (as all the gear is) out to the floor in front of the stage. This push could be a matter of feet or (in some cases) a hundred yards through an alley and up to a window on the second floor. It just depends on the building and what it has available.

"There are three distinct and different crews that make up a tour: the lighting crew, the sound crew, and the band's personal crew who set up and take care of their band gear, guitars, and the like. These band aides, as they are sometimes called, also include the production manager, stage manager, and overall tour manager (who usually travels with the band and deals with all of their needs).

"The call for band crew is usually about noon or one o'clock. They are the last in and the first out (which can definitely cause tension). After all, the rest of the crew has been hard at work for quite a while. Once the band gear is placed and checked, the lights focused, and sound gear tested, we have what is known as a *sound check.* This usually happens around three in the afternoon, and can run anywhere from ten minutes to three hours. Sometimes the band crew (usually musicians themselves) will play the gear for this. If not, this can make for an ugly sound check for those of us forced to listen. By five in the evening the lights are done, providing they all worked. This is not to be held against the light crew. The gear is delicate, and its being trucked and handled on a daily basis takes its toll on even the toughest of gear. The PA is up and running now, and if you think you can take a break—you're wrong. The opening act has yet to set up, and all their gear has to be miked, and tested and then a sound check conducted. Band gear, stage monitors, and other equipment will all have to be struck from the stage or moved to accommodate the new gear so that there is room for the act. This is usually finished and wrapped up around seven or so in the evening. Doors to the house are now open, and any work you have to do at this point is done with the crowd present. Fun, huh?

"Depending on your job, you may or may not have to work during the show. The band crew will be all over the stage changing guitars, and at least one senior light technician will be there. Anything that breaks during the show—you have to fix it during the show. This is most stressful on the band crew—because though you might be able to do the show with a few less lights, it's pretty hard to pull off if the lead guitar's rig goes down. A couple of screwups by the band crew during a show usually gets you an early plane ticket home. Any production manager worth his salt has got a long list of band-gear technicians who are always ready to replace you for less money than what you are making.

"Once the show is over, you are moving quickly. You could have as many as two to ten tractor-trailers' worth full of gear that is hanging from the ceiling or on the stage, and the trucks all have to come down and be loaded. This is the hardest part of the day because it is a fast and furious pace, and road crews take exceptional pride in their load-out times. Usually by two in the morning, the gear is back on the trucks and the crew bus is waiting. Now it is on to the next city because the next show loads in at eight in the morning. Enjoy.

"Throughout the entire day, there is an unseen dance going on between stagehands, lighting and sound crew, the band crew, and promoter representatives. Everyone knows the dance and performs it without even thinking, until a new face shows up that hasn't danced before. One inexperienced person can cause more damage and bodily harm than any other single factor on the road. They trip over cables and even guitars. They put things where they don't belong, don't know who to ask for help, and are usually in the way. If you are new on the road . . . keep a low profile (that means that you stay low and let us make the profile) and do *exactly* what you are told. As the years go by, you will learn the dance and hopefully won't have gotten anybody killed in the process. You will also learn who *not* to talk to during the day. Most road people have been doing this sort of thing for years and know everyone at the halls you will be playing. They have earned a reputation (some good and some bad), but no one wants to hear from the new kid. The day is too short and the hours too long. Ask a million questions to your immediate supervisor but that is about the length of it in the beginning. Watch and learn. Nothing is done without a reason, no matter how trivial it may seem. There just isn't time for anything else."

Expert Advice

"We get an incredible feeling from seeing and hearing a crowd jump on its feet and scream. It's our job satisfaction to know that without us, none of it would have been possible. The best way to make the impossible happen with us is to tell us that it can't be done. Not only will we show you that it can be, but it can be done better than you had hoped. We don't get our names in lights and we don't care about that. There is no limousine waiting for us. We don't want to be stars or hang out with stars. We just do our job and go home to the family. We don't broadcast to people what we do for a living because we don't want to answer the same dumb question every place we go. What's it like? What's it like? What's it like? The answer is—we simply love what we do."

INTERVIEW
Randall Presswood
Director of Performing Arts Facilities

Randall Presswood serves as director of performing arts facilities for Bloomsburg University in Bloomsburg, Pennsylvania. He earned a Bachelor of Arts in technical theater from Coe College in Cedar Rapids, Iowa, and an M.F.A. in theater design/lighting from Wayne State University in Detroit. He served his internship as assistant technical director at the Chelsea Theatre Center in New York City.

How Randall Presswood Got Started

"My theater 'bug' developed from having performed and worked in the technical aspect of theater at my high school in Wentzville, Missouri. I enjoyed the challenge of solving (technical) problems for short-run productions that would enthrall, dazzle, or amaze the audiences. I delighted in seeing the satisfaction and joy on the faces of the audiences as they left the theater, having escaped for two hours from the worries and stress of their everyday routines. I enjoyed the recognition I received for being part of a successful production, and the great comfort and camaraderie I felt from my 'extended family.' I knew that what I felt is what I wanted for the audiences, too, that came to my productions. I believe that theater gave me the opportunity to make a small statement to society and to perhaps make a positive impact on the lives of those who witnessed my efforts. It wasn't necessary for them to know that I had a part in this process—it was enough for me to know.

"Choosing theater as a career and lifestyle would allow me to experience this feeling day-in and day-out. For me, there was clearly no other choice."

What the Job's Really Like

"As the director of a performing arts facility, I now not only have the opportunity to provide this joy for the patrons of my own productions, but I also am able to provide a venue for other theater professionals and for amateurs alike to present their work to the public. Thus I am able to continue this cycle of escape and entertainment: allowing others to fulfill their own dreams of providing joy for the theater-going public.

"I enjoyed the creativity offered me in technical theater (particularly lighting design) more than I did performing. So I decided to study lighting design, with the dream of one day accepting the Tony for outstanding lighting design (I still have my acceptance speech ready). I designed for the college and university I attended as much as possible, and insisted that I be allowed to design a production (with no additional pay) each time I took a summer job as a theater-technician/gofer. As I studied the field, I did everything I could—performing, designing, assisting, drafting—to enhance my experience. My intent was just to be a part of any type of theater that was happening wherever I was. As a result, I received a tremendous amount of education and experience. I learned what was needed as an actor to 'find the light,' what was needed to produce the light as a designer and electrician, and what was needed to make scenery safe, secure, pleasing, and exciting. I also learned what it took to produce a costume on the stage and what was necessary to manage the stage during a production run. Everything I did added to a total education that has made it possible for me to conduct the business of directing a performing arts facility.

"After receiving my Master of Fine Arts degree in lighting, I accepted a position as a university technical director (with lighting-design responsibilities). One of my first responsibilities was to refurbish the production shop of this university. I had to research and specify the replacement or purchase of all hand and stationary or portable power tools. Later (for this same university), I was charged with designing a student computer laboratory and with refurbishing the rigging, sound systems, and lighting instrumentation and control, as well as with designing a production space for a summer dinner theater (complete with preparation kitchen and wet bar). What a wonderful world this opened up for me! I was no longer confined to the benefits of only my designs, but now every designer who ventured after me would benefit from my planning and specifications.

"When I left this particular university in upstate New York, I sought an opportunity to continue with refurbishing facilities. What I found instead was a performing arts center just under construction in northern California. Being hired as the production manager, I was responsible for the production shop from the ground up. (It was literally four walls when I arrived.) Every tool and cabinet was of my specification. The Center had hired a theater consultant and sound consultant to assist in the construction of the facility. So although I was not responsible for specifying lighting or sound, my association with these consultants was again a tremendous learning opportunity. My knowledge base was growing by leaps and bounds. I was now familiar and experienced with lighting systems, stage carpentry, electrical needs, safety and fire codes, security needs and applications, budgets, savings methods, personnel and employment procedures, janitorial methods, supplies, and much more. I had developed a large vendor file and was able to make quick and efficient deals. In short, I was building a reputation (not a world-renowned one as I had hoped to forge on Broadway as a lighting designer, but a regional one as a manager who could get the job done, whatever the job was). I freelanced as a lighting designer, scenic designer, costumer, and I joined Actors' Equity Association as a stage manager.

"As production manager for the Center in California, I scheduled the facilities for in-house productions as well as the outside rentals. I created the policies and procedures that outside groups would follow to use in their facilities. Eventually I began to field calls from other regional centers in the area, wanting to know how I handled this situation or that one, where they should buy this type of hardware, who is the best supplier for lighting equipment, and so forth. My name continued to grow. I was no longer a lighting designer, but now a theater designer.

"When I left California, I knew that I would have to continue in my new career—theater design. It wasn't that my career path had changed (after all, I was still a working theater professional), but it had evolved into what I had actually been trained for. All of my experiences contributed to one another, and my path as a theater designer (I see in hindsight) seemed inevitable. It is these experiences, as much as my training, that landed me in my current position in central Pennsylvania as the director of performing arts facilities for Bloomsburg University.

"I am fortunate that in my present position, my supervisors understand the impact and needs of my position. They assist me in helping them present more opportunities for the users of my facilities. It is not a 'piece of cake,' however.

"I spend a great deal of time scheduling the facilities I direct for the many users who wish access. I am charged by my superiors to provide the most opportunities possible. I run two venues (a six-hundred-seat hall and two-thousand-seat hall), and I average four classes and four performances or dress rehearsals per day in my facilities (scheduled a year in advance). I often have to determine the needs of these users, as they may well be novices in the theater and not only unfamiliar with theatrical terminology but also unaware of what can be accomplished in a producing venue. I have to tread the fine line of not offering too much and, in so doing, overwhelming the user, but offering enough so as to provide for the user the best production possible. As the facility director, I am required to review each technical rider for outside presenters or touring groups being produced by the institution. I may choose to contact the proposed group and negotiate the technical needs of the presentation. Although much of this can be accomplished through e-mail and other electronic means, it can nonetheless become quite time-consuming.

"Depending upon the performance season, I employ twelve to thirty assistants. Each of these employees must be trained in the general theatrical amenities of my facilities, as well as in the specific control and operation of the facility's technology (lighting and sound) and in procedures and policies for my department and the institution as a whole. The security of my equipment, the safety of my employees, and the safety of the users and patrons depend on the knowledge I provide these employees. Because of the time demands on my venues, this training is often done at the performances—which then requires my attendance. It is not unusual to work an eighteen-hour day or to work four to six weeks straight without a full day off. It is typical to be called in for an hour or two during a weekend off. The general workday, however, would be about eight to ten hours daily, Monday through Friday. A well-trained staff will determine the availability of my time off.

"As an administrator I spend between four and eight hours per week in meetings. It is expected that I will likewise spend time contributing to the community.

"Another large portion of my day (and one, in fact, consuming most of my thoughts while away from the office) is spent planning for improvements, facility rehabilitation, equipment upgrades and replacement, and general maintenance. Since much of this work must be performed by professionals and union tradespeople, a good deal of advance planning and paperwork is required. I must anticipate my needs and my facility and equipment failures in order to schedule these around rentals and productions, which are generating income for the institution. To accomplish this I must spend time researching and keeping abreast of current and proposed technology and theater trends, attending workshops, seminars, and conferences to gain this knowledge. This planning then increases my employee base as I become the site supervisor for the contractors hired to complete the projects placed into the schedule. Gaining the funding for these projects may require grant writing. Of course, while all of this work and preparation is going on, the eight events per day also are continuing. Everything in my job is deadline-based. The stage must be cleared and set by a certain time, the lights must be focused and cued by an exact time, and so forth. The audience will enter the doors at 6 P.M. whether you are prepared for them or not.

Consequently, you simply must be prepared, no matter what, no matter when. I have found that a good sense of humor and the ability to let things roll off your back are essential for an arts-facilities director.

"What I like most about my job is its constantly changing nature. Although I may do the same or similar work day after day, it is always for a new client with a new set of needs. The challenges are never ending, and the solutions to these challenges carry immediate and gratifying rewards. I am in a visible position. My success results in an increased demand on my time and talents. The more I am able to accomplish in my own venue, the more other venues come to me for advice or consultation. I accept this as a compliment and reward for my hard work. I am particularly pleased to be working for an institution that values my efforts, opinions, and proposals; one that goes the extra step to secure the funding necessary for me to be successful. This is not always the case, so I feel rewarded to have that support and encouragement.

"Of course, the sometimes relentless hours and the need to occasionally function under 'crisis management' are among the dislikes of my job. As an administrator I am sometimes viewed as the obstacle or enemy to those presenting in my venue. It is my job to provide a total experience for many users and patrons. However, each user is convinced that their four hours in my space is the most important thing I will do all year. When I thoroughly research and propose a project and become convinced that it is an important step for the institution, it is indeed frustrating when I am unable to convince my superiors to share that belief. Whereas the art of theater is a collaborative one, the business of theater is often tooth and nail."

Expert Advice

"If you want to make a living in theater, be prepared to go where the path leads you. Don't force yourself down the straight path when the winding one is tugging at your bootstraps. If it is important to you to be a theater professional, then just be in the theater. Don't insist that you become an actor or designer. Be willing (and prepared) to become a box office manager, stage carpenter, or a director of performing arts facilities."

INTERVIEW
Dennis Parichy
Lighting Designer

Dennis Parichy earned a Bachelor of Science degree in theater from the School of Speech at Northwestern University in Evanston, Illinois. In addition, he completed course work in lighting design, drafting, drawing, and painting for the theater designer at the Lester Polakov Studio and Forum of Stage Design. He serves as a professional lighting designer.

How Dennis Parichy Got Started

"My first designs were for Eagles Mere Playhouse in Eagles Mere, Pennsylvania, a non-Equity summer theater operated by Alvina Krause, professor of acting at Northwestern University. I discovered lighting design in a class in stage lighting during my junior year at Northwestern University, and was so fascinated that I asked Miss Krause to take me to Eagles Mere (she took people she judged to be talented and trainable) so that I could try this new field. Previously I had flirted with writing plays, acting (too self-conscious), and technical theater, about which I knew very little. So since lighting seemed an important and fascinating area of theater, I wanted to try my hand at it. Working at Eagles Mere—nine shows in ten weeks—I was an electrician as well as a designer, and other than some aid from the directors, it was all up to me, without supervision or help. Consequently, I had to take the ideas that lighting class had given me about technique and craft (with the injunction to support and illuminate the play) and try to work out how to light each show effectively and artistically. This included a substantial amount of trial and error, in addition to putting Professor Theodore Fuch's teachings into practice. The only experience I had had before this was working on the lighting crew for a couple of university productions.

"In the course of three summers, I learned an enormous amount about turning lighting ideas into effective designs. I had to test each idea I had acquired, figure out how to make it work with limited resources, find out what worked and what did not, and discover my own lighting preferences. It was, of course, a high-pressure situation guided only by my own insights and the needs of the moment. So compared with formal training, it was chaotic, but it gave me invaluable experience about the realities of achieving a lighting design. I was able to learn firsthand how you must light the actors and the space effectively in order to achieve the basic goal of making the theatrical performance visible to the audience in a way that helps them understand and relate to the onstage events.

"For several years, I had been interested in astronomy, physics, and engineering as possible careers. All these areas fascinated me, though I never felt I had the necessary drive and kind of mind that could carry me far in those professions. But looking back, I would say that those interests predisposed me to find lighting design (which has apparent technical aspects—control, instrumentation, optics, color—all concrete and gadget-like things) a familiar and exciting field. The other influence was totally nontechnical: a great fascination with books (primarily stories—novels, adventures), which briefly led me into playwriting. I had an interest in stories and the telling of stories, which is what theater does. So theater design, and specifically lighting, combined an interest in technical and scientific things with the opportunity to help tell fascinating stories about people's experiences, to put those technical things in the service of creating art."

What the Job's Really Like

"Once the rudiments of technique are acquired, lighting design involves the ability to delve into the nature of a script, libretto, score, or choreography; to open your mind to what it is, what it means, what emotions, images, and ideas it evokes in you; and to translate those things into ideas about color, direction, and intensity of light. The job has four major components:

1. Experiencing the work. This includes reading a script, listening to a score, watching a rehearsal in order to

experience the work for yourself in some vivid and immediate way. It means exploring the ideas, images, and emotions this experience arouses in you and developing your own point of view about the piece at hand. The process may require a single reading or listening or a dozen or more, depending on the particular show, its complexity and demands, and your own interest and needs.

2. Discussing the work. The next stage focuses on discussions with the show's director or producer, the other designers, and anyone else involved in creating the overall production. This usually requires several meetings or phone conversations with one or several of your fellow collaborators, all in pursuit of defining the needs of this particular production regarding lighting, scenic, costume, and directorial elements. The goal is to produce a unified approach to the play in which the lighting design will blend with and support the work of everyone else. This process takes place over the course of several weeks.

3. Arranging the lighting instruments. Once the first two steps are well underway (they may continue and overlap with later stages of your work), you take the ideas and needs and points of view about the show and sit down at the drafting table, desk, and computer to figure out (in very specific terms) how to arrange lighting instruments in the theater space to create the kind of look that you and the director have decided the show should have. This means analyzing the scenic elements; the physical reality of the theater; the money, time, and resources available to you. Then you determine and solve the inherent problems in this particular situation. During this part of the process, you have to decide what kind of lights you need (or how to use those available), where to put them, where they will be focused, how to control them, and what color and intensity they must have in order to achieve your goals. The designer then has to produce a light plot, hookup, shop order, and other lists and specifications that will communicate to his crew what he needs, where it should be located in the theater,

and how it will be wired and equipped. This part of the job may be done by the designer himself in the studio or with assistants. It can last anywhere from a day or two to three weeks (for a large and complex show) and may require constant consultation with the producers, managers, and the shops that supply the equipment, and the men who do the installation.

4. Creating the lighting. The last phase of lighting design is the actual week to several weeks you spend in the theater creating the specific lighting and executing the design to make the show have the look everyone has decided upon. This begins when the lights are hung, and it includes focusing the lights, creating the looks of the show (the cues), rehearsing the show, and modifying and refining the looks so that they all help the audience experience the show. Most of the time this period lasts from two to three days for summer stock to about ten days for most regional theater shows and most plays. In the case of new and complex musicals, however, the time required may be several weeks of putting in twelve-hour days, six days a week.

"A typical day is difficult to spell out since every show has its own schedule, needs, and special circumstances. In the professional theater, most designers are in the process of designing several shows at once, each at a different stage of the process. So a typical day might easily involve working in the studio in the morning on the light plot or hookup of a show you are going to do in two or three weeks. Then in the afternoon you might go to a run-through of the show that you will light next week. During the rehearsal, you note important things about cuing and staging that must be taken into account. You may discuss specific cues, problems, or needs with the stage manager and director. At the end of rehearsal you might be required to attend a production meeting about a show that you will do two months later and discuss with the director and perhaps other designers various ideas about that show, what its story is, and what it should look like. And then in the evening—if you're very busy and the schedule is tight (as it often is)—you either go home and read the script for another show or think about the show just discussed or go to the theater and begin focusing on next week's show (till midnight, typically).

"There are of course an infinite number of variations on this schedule. The designer is required to take control of his or her work, to be self-motivated, independent, dedicated, and ambitious. You have to get the job done, and no one is supervising you.

"The work, while you're working, is intense, often tense, and driven by deadlines. The plot has to be delivered on time, the lights have to go in the theater on a specific day, and there can be no postponements. You have to be ready, and you have to be willing and able to work under pressure and to take charge. Once in a while it is relaxed and easygoing, but that is the exception. Most lighting designers, in order to make a good living, take on as many shows as they can possibly work into their schedules, so high pressure, anxiety, and stress are inevitable parts of the experience.

"I have often had the privilege and opportunity to work with playwrights, directors, designers, and actors who welcome my contribution and with whom I have forged lasting personal and artistic relationships. But sometimes shows are fraught with disagreement, demands, and unhappiness, and these situations can be stressful and exhausting. Each show is a new challenge and adventure.

"What I like most about my work is the chance to help create an effective theatrical event in collaboration with other eager, exciting, and stimulating theater artists. The process of creating the design—especially the days in the theater—is almost always an exciting and satisfying time, because it gives me a chance to exercise my skills and visual talents, which is immensely satisfying. The process, from show to show, may be bumpy or difficult or fraught with occasional conflict. But in the end it is almost always such a source of fulfillment that this makes the difficulties acceptable.

"The downside of lighting design (applicable I believe to almost all theatrical careers) is that there is often a lack of continuity, security, and stability in theatrical work. No matter how advanced your career, there is always the possibility that you may have to struggle for sufficient work to support yourself and a family. As associates and colleagues move on in their careers, you may have to unexpectedly develop new relationships and find new sources of work. Since the network of friends and professional colleagues—especially directors—is extremely important to one's success, you are often vulnerable to significant changes in your relationships with theaters and other theater artists. At some point, finding work that will stimulate and stretch your artistic muscles may be difficult, and you have to be continually aware of the need to escape from the typecasting that inevitably happens and of the need to find ways to expand your horizons."

Expert Advice

"The most important advice I could give someone interested in lighting design as a career is to be realistic about the probable monetary and artistic rewards of lighting design in the theater. If you have the dedication, drive, and ambition to tackle the professional world, to put in the inevitable apprenticeship learning the ropes and living hand-to-mouth for a while, you have a chance. If you are determined to do it and are willing to brave the rigors of finding your niche, you have a good chance of succeeding. Training is important, but dedication and enthusiasm, a willingness to learn and expand, a genuine enjoyment of and eagerness to work with and for others, and an effort to submit your artistic impulses to the needs and demands of the production are what will make you a success."

INTERVIEW
Twyla Mitchell
Costume Shop Teaching Assistant, Stage Manager

Twyla Mitchell is currently working as a costume shop teaching assistant as a method of paying for graduate school, but she has also worked as a stage manager. Currently in her second year of a combined M.A.-Ph.D. program at the University of California in Santa Barbara, she earned her Bachelor of Arts Degree in drama from the University of California in Irvine. She also completed internships with the Pacific Conservatory of the Performing Arts in Santa Maria, California, and with Western Stage in Salinas, California.

How Twyla Mitchell Got Started

"I feel that educational theater is important on so many levels. First of all, it's one of the last remnants of truly experimental theater. While universities are concerned with making money, economics isn't as all-consuming an issue in them as it is in the other forms of theater. Even students who do not go forth into the theater hopefully can come out with an appreciation for all it can mean—for the importance of art in a culture that so often seems to have forgotten it. On a more personal level, a professorship is likely to be a significantly more stable position than any other in theater."

What the Job's Really Like

"As a graduate student, the time constraints are enormous. For example, in addition to the regular reading required in seminars, it is assumed that you will participate in some sort of side reading—further research on that week's topic, enabling you to come to class with some significant contribution to add to the discussion. Furthermore, it is assumed that you are doing some sort of practically oriented side project, which can take anywhere from ten to thirty hours of your week, depending on the scope of your involvement. In addition there is usually some sort of teaching assistantship, which occupies another twenty hours of your week. So in a slow week you'll spend forty hours on various projects. In a typical week, it's in the fifty- to sixty-hour range. And for a hectic week (say, nearing paper deadlines or performance times) it often gets into the eighty- to one-hundred-hour range.

"The atmosphere varies with the time pressure; often everyone goes through similar constraints, and the support level will vary with your colleagues. In a highly competitive atmosphere there can be great levels of tension, like in any workplace, while in a more cooperative environment there can be a strong sense of everyone's being in the same boat, which can be a greater help to one's sometimes-precarious sanity than it would seem.

"I really love the classes I am teaching in the basic elements of costume building. I never get tired of them. I don't even mind when I have to repeat the explanation two or three times. (Good thing, because that happens a lot!) I also really love studying, researching, finding out things I never knew before and that maybe other people never knew before, and trying to find clear precise ways of explaining them.

"The downside is that there aren't enough hours in the week to do all that and yet spend time with my toddler, so I often find myself stretched terribly thin. I have tried to find shortcuts when I can. For example, I do a great deal of research on the Internet and often check out books (in the one-hour blocks I get during the day) to take home and look over after my child is in bed, but I still am forced to make many sacrifices in my attempt to reconcile all of these elements.

"I would advise others to read as much as they can—not just plays but also criticism and theory. Absorb all you can, whenever you can. Talk to people 'in the know' and glean as much knowledge as you can from them.

"As far as being a stage manager, I've always been fascinated with stage managers: professionals who know everything about what's going on and who get to call the shots. They seem to be the final authority on many issues.

"Working as a stage manager, I have found that a typical day usually involves meetings—small meetings with each department or a huge meeting with all the designers and shop heads to discuss the progress of the upcoming show. Once a show has opened, it's small check-in meetings with the actors, crew, crew heads, and others, to see how things are flowing, how they are being maintained, what problems are on the horizon, and so forth. Then the stage manager acts as secretary, types up and distributes the notes from the formal meetings so that everyone has a clear picture of what is being discussed and developed.

"The latter part of the day or evening usually involves either rehearsals or performances, or both, with the stage manager's acting in any of a number of different roles (e.g., stage hands, assistants), depending on the size and scope of the theater and the production and the stage manager's working relationship with the director.

"The best part of being a stage manager is that you really have the opportunity to be in on all elements of the production, from the concept meeting forward to postshow strike. You get to work with some truly amazing artists across the board and form a complete notion of the process. The downside is the fact that the buck stops with you. As with all middle management, you are the one to whom the producers turn when a problem comes up, and you had best have a way of solving it. It can create a tremendous feeling of overload and pressure, which is why stage managers have a very high burnout rate. To paraphrase a cliché, when everything is going wrong, everyone blames you, and when everything is going well, nobody notices you."

Expert Advice

"Learn all you can about the different aspects in theater: costumes, props, light, sound, acting, directing, and so forth. The more you know, the more effectively you can communicate with the artists you will be working with. It's also a good idea to brush up on your self-confidence and self-esteem, because both can sometimes take a beating out there."

INTERVIEW
Mark T. Simpson
Lighting Designer

Mark T. Simpson earned his Bachelor of Arts degree from Case Western Reserve University in Cleveland, Ohio, and a Master of Arts degree from the American University in Washington, DC in interdisciplinary studies (lighting and set design for the theater). He is now completing his M.F.A. in lighting design at New York University's Tisch School of the Arts. He also served an internship as stage manager at the Cleveland Play House in Cleveland, Ohio, and is now employed as a lighting designer.

How Mark T. Simpson Got Started

"For me, theater is exciting, interesting, and immediate. I first set foot in a theater my senior year of college. I took beginning acting for an 'easy A' and signed up for running crew for an extra credit. Sitting behind the light board during a performance one night, it suddenly occurred to me that people get paid to do this! I no longer had a choice, I was hooked. I didn't know exactly what I could do in the theater, but I knew it would be theater. It was the only place I'd ever been where the prospect of spending my time and exerting my energies didn't seem like intolerable drudgery. The theater was also filled with the nicest, most selfless people I had ever met. The stereotypical egomaniacal actors were few and far between, and usually they were young and not destined to last long. The professionals who had been in the business for years and years were all wonderful—Jonathan Hadary, Daniel J. Travanti, Tammy Grimes. I was lucky to work with them early, as guest artists, and during my internship at the Cleveland Play House.

"Lighting design turned out to be something that addressed all of my talents and inclinations: technology, art, special relations, mathematics and physics, computers, and robotics. Lastly, theater as an art appealed to me politically and socially. It is an optimist's art form: people can be changed and educated by peaceful demonstrations of opinions and alternatives. It is a pacifist's art form: it provides a socially acceptable outlet to explore and cathartically deal with violence and negativity, and it never has the intention to harm the participants or the audience. It is an art form for people seeking to live healthy, whole, productive, creative lives."

What the Job's Really Like

"My typical day involves at least eight hours of doing something else that's not my career. When I'm in New York, I work a full day as a temp, doing clerical or computer work. If I'm the resident designer for an equity summer theater, I'm also a carpenter. If it's turnover time and I'm actually working on lights, I'm an electrician. Over the summer, I work three 40-hour weeks and one 100-hour week. Out of those 220 hours, I spend about eighteen hours as a lighting designer. Back in New York, I did eight shows in the last eight months. In one month, I worked 176 hours at my day job and fifty hours in a theater. Of those 226 hours, about twenty are designing lights. So, on the average, I have to work about ten hours for the privilege of working just an hour on my career.

"My work as a lighting designer comprises about eight hours' drafting and doing paperwork, three hours in meetings, and eight to fifteen hours in rehearsals, writing the light cues, taking notes, and making corrections. It is the last eight to fifteen hours in the theater that keep me coming back. It is busy, tense, but not negative. I often am convinced that it's impossible to finish in time for opening, but I always do. I sometimes find myself crawling along duct work twenty feet off the floor or balancing a 200-pound pipe on a hydraulic lift twenty feet off the floor, but that is work that will go away once I reach the top of my profession.

"Being a lighting designer isn't dangerous, but getting there is. The work atmosphere is very positive. When you get in the theater and see a moment of magic on the stage that is a direct result of your effort and imagination, you hear immediate approval from your peers, and your spine tingles with the realization that this personal success of yours adds to the value of everyone else's work. And when an audience responds to it, your spine tingles again.

"What I like most are the people, the creativity, using ingenuity, solving problems, and the short-term nature of projects. What I like least are the low pay, understaffing, underbudgeting, lack of time allotted for first-class work, and the poor public understanding of what constitutes high-quality work."

Expert Advice

"If you have to do this, you'll know it. Just show up and work hard. If you can, go to Yale or New York University; if you can't, don't give up. Visit with a number of other designers, decide what you like, and imitate it until you understand it. Take chances with your work. Make big statements as often as you can. Pay attention to the whole first, the details second. Leave yourself time to finish your designs: finished-and-modest is better than unfinished-and-grandiose. Draw every day. Paint every day. Draft every day. Have fun—why else would you be in this business?"

INTERVIEW
David Palmer
Theater Manager

David Palmer serves as theater manager of the Ruth B. Shannon Center for the Performing Arts at Whittier College in Whittier, California. He earned an Associates Degree in Business at Delta College in Bay City, Michigan, a Bachelor of Arts from California State University in Long Beach, and both a Master of Arts and a Master of Fine Arts in stage lighting design from California State University in Long Beach. He also served two years at Michigan State University, touring with the "Ball of Yarns" Children's Theater Company, and he also toured and taught in Lansing Public Schools with the "Lansing Team of Four" Creative Dramatics Troupe. Other positions include theater manager/lighting designer at the University of Houston, Texas, and technical director at the University of South Carolina, in Columbia. Within California Palmer was lighting designer/master electrician at the Grove Shakespeare Festival in Garden Grove, lighting designer/technical director at Santa Ana College, lighting designer/instructor at CSU Long Beach Department of Theater, lighting designer/technical director at the CSU Long Beach Department of Dance, and cofounder/lighting designer for the Alternative Repertory Theatre in Santa Ana, and lighting designer at Shakespeare Orange County.

How David Palmer Got Started

"In high school, I worked in the audiovisual department during my free periods. Among my duties were to run the sound for basketball games and to set up lighting and sound for the dances in the gym following the game. My experience in theater had been zero! But I found that I enjoyed the work.

"Some time later, a very close friend convinced me to help on a summer production of a Gilbert and Sullivan operetta at the local community theater. I spent most of my time in the scene shop helping build the sets—never having had formal training, just doing what I had watched my father do in our home woodshop. I found that I really enjoyed the work, the pace of activity, the sense of accomplishment, and creating the 'magic' of perception versus reality (what the audience sees versus what is behind the scenes).

"It wasn't until I had transferred from a junior college to a four-year institution that I found out that I could actually take classes in theater, that there was such a thing as a theater major, and that one could make a living at it. After one quarter, I changed majors from business administration to theater. Since that time, I have been making a living *and* performing work I enjoy.

"Another milestone in my career occurred when I was given an opportunity to travel to California to design the lighting for a touring opera, and I discovered the plethora of work that was available. Still other milestones occurred when I transferred to CSU-Long Beach to finish my B.A. and then proceeded to earn my M.A. and M.F.A. This program was simply outstanding, and it provided significant professional training, contacts, and teaching experience. All of the jobs that I have had since coming out to California twenty years ago have been a direct result of the contacts that I began to establish when I transferred to CSU-LB."

What the Job's Really Like

"My job now is very administrative. I spend much of my time on the telephone with artists, managers, printers, possible crew members, potential and current donors, and so forth. I divide my time between booking and artist services, box-office supervision, marketing and public relations, technical preparations, and performances. On any given day, the proportion among them all changes. Some days are very laid-back and relaxed. Others just don't have enough hours in them.

"The job isn't really dangerous, unless you have a heart condition. I typically put in nine to twelve hours a day, six to seven days per week during the academic year (September 1 to May 25). The summer is a fairly normal nine-to-five type of job with fewer performances.

"Since all but one of the staff are students here at the college, I try to maintain a professional yet educational work environment. I find that I will spend ten or fifteen minutes explaining the why of a question to students and helping them reach solutions based on their own knowledge, rather than giving a definitive 'yes' or 'no' type of answer. The workplace is another classroom. As a result, the amount of work accomplished is often less than in a fully professional environment. But the students are gaining an understanding of a profession that is often perceived as being all-play-and-no-work. In the end, many of the artists and patrons who visit the Shannon Center are simply not aware that everyone on the crew is an undergraduate student.

"First and foremost, I like watching the glow of an audience member's face as he or she exits the theater after a first-rate performance. I feel that I have helped accomplish something for each one of those individuals. Second (but not by much) is watching the expression of understanding light up in a student's eyes who suddenly discovers a new piece of information with real-life application. After that, I enjoy meeting and working with all of the people—artists, patrons, students, staff. We are all in this together. This is a business of emotions, not just dollar signs. Everything has a human value associated with it."

Expert Advice

"In order to be successful in this (or any) business, you must have a passion for what you do. That passion will help you strive for the best, 100 percent of the time. An attitude of 'that's good enough' just isn't acceptable. Being an idealist capable of thinking in a geometric or nonlinear fashion is a big plus. Taking an idea, rolling it around and coming up with four more ideas that then spark still four more ideas is how you come up with fresh and exciting events. Never say no until you have exhausted all the possibilities, because if you really want something, you will find a way of doing it. Finally, always remember that 'what goes around, comes around.' The favor that you do for someone else will come back to you, just when you need it most. I have found that it has worked for me since the early 1970s when I did that favor for my friend and helped him out with the Gilbert and Sullivan operetta."

FOR MORE INFORMATION

The following companies and associations can provide additional information and possibilities for career advancement.

Acoustical Society of America (ASA)
500 Sunnyside Boulevard
Woodbury, NY 11797

American Theater Works, Inc.
Theater Directories
P.O. Box 519
Dorset, VT 05251

Arista Records
6 West 57th Street
New York, NY 10019
Contact: Human Resources

Association for Communication Administration
ACA National Office
311 Wilson Hall
Murray State University
Murray, KY 42071

Broadcast Education Association
National Association of Broadcasters
1771 N Street, NW
Washington, DC 20006

Cleopatra Records
P.O. Box 1394
Hollywood, CA 90078

International Alliance of Theatrical Stage Employees (IATSE)
Local 33 IATSE
1720 West Magnolia Boulevard
Burbank, CA 91506

International Association of Auditorium Managers (IAAM)
4425 West Airport Freeway
Irving, TX 75062

International Brotherhood of Electrical Workers (IBEW)
1125 15th Street NW
Washington, DC 20005

National Association of Broadcasters
Employment Clearinghouse
1771 N Street, NW
Washington, DC 20036

National Association of Schools of Theater
11250 Roger Bacon Drive, Suite 21
Reston, VA 22090

SONY Music and Entertainment, Inc.
550 Madison Avenue, 2nd Floor
New York, NY 10022-3211
Contact: Recruitment Department

CHAPTER 5 The Business of Entertainment

EDUCATION
B.A./B.S. or formal training
recommended

$$$ SALARY/EARNINGS
$18,000 to $60,000 and up

OVERVIEW

Music

In the world at large, the art of negotiation by a third party has existed ever since individuals began communicating with one another. This job of "facilitator" was historically given to the individual who, for a fee, would arrange an audience with important officials (or royalty) or set up a meeting for those seeking a face-to-face encounter. Today, in the world of entertainment, this job is often handled by individuals called personal managers, business managers, booking agents, or artists' agents who act as representatives and negotiators for their clients.

Are you knowledgeable about the world of music but uncomfortable in performing? Do you have a desire to handle the business end of things? Can you speak persuasively? Are you good with figures? You might be interested in becoming an artist's representative, personal manager, or booking agent.

ARTISTS' REPRESENTATIVES PERSONAL/BUSINESS MANAGERS Personal managers, also called artists' representatives, are responsible for representing artists. Their specific responsibilities may vary, but often they are in charge of all aspects of a music performer's career, promoting the client's interests whenever and wherever possible. This includes business decisions and may even include all or some creative decisions.

An agent may represent many artists at one time. Sometimes an agent specializes and represents only one type of performer or even one type of music, such as rock music. He or she may work for a large or small agency or be self-employed.

Much of an agent's time is spent on the phone, fax, or with e-mail, discussing prospects, arranging meetings, making networking connections, and keeping in touch with what is going on in the industry. One of the most important jobs for agents is to negotiate contracts. Other duties include seeing to and improving costuming, choreography, backup musicians and tunes; arranging publicity; and providing guidance for their client performers. If the entertainer is well established, the manager may be in charge of support personnel, including publicists or public relations firms, road personnel, security people, accountants, producers, musicians, and merchandisers. Successful managers are always in constant communication with the act's booking agent or agency.

Booking agents are also called theatrical agents, booking managers, booking representatives, agents, or bookers. These professionals are in charge of arranging engagements for both solo musical artists and groups for movies, television programming, concerts, and other live performances. They usually represent a number of clients at a time. Sometimes they are chosen to act as talent buyers for concert halls or clubs or may open their own talent agency.

Business managers concentrate on the financial affairs of the singers, musicians, and other entertainers whom they represent. They are often the ones who negotiate with agents or representatives for contracts and appearances. They may also negotiate with television producers, record companies, and motion picture studios, and they sometimes seek large endorsements of concert tours. They are in charge of all fiscal disbursements, making sure the bills are in order and that the payroll for all employees in the act (including road personnel, musicians, vocalists, publicists, public relations firms, lawyers) is dispensed properly. Some business managers may even be in charge of the artist's personal bills.

Acting

PRODUCERS Producers are entrepreneurs who have financial and administrative control over the making of movies, plays, and television shows. It is their responsibility to raise enough money, oversee all finances, and make sure that all dollars are wisely spent. They must find investors (called "angels") who are willing to put up money to finance the project. They are the ones who are ultimately responsible for turning a profit for the investors. The producer is also responsible for selecting the plays or scripts, deciding on the size and content of the production, and determining its budget.

Scripts may be located in a number of ways. Playwrights may send them to producers, producers might also do new versions of previous productions, and often producers may commission a playwright to write a script. Once a script is located or written, the producer will pay the playwright for an option to use the script for a specified time period.

Producers also hire directors who make the artistic and day-to-day decisions on the production. They also choose the principal members of the cast and key production staff members. They may negotiate contracts with artistic personnel (often in accordance with collective bargaining agreements) and coordinate the activities of writers, directors, managers, and other personnel. Producers have many responsibilities: ultimately they are the ones who make the decisions that determine the success of the project.

Television producers are employed by television stations or networks. Network television series usually have an executive producer who does the long-term planning for the show. Movie producers are employed by a film studio or may work independently. Theatrical producers work independently.

CASTING DIRECTORS Casting directors are influential theater professionals who audition and interview performers for specific parts in a play or movie. In order to correctly match people with parts, casting directors read scripts and then work with others of the production staff to determine their thoughts, ideas, and desires regarding the character's personality, voice quality, and physical appearance.

Casting directors can find the right performers in a number of ways. They develop advertisements and place them in the trade newspapers or other publications. These ads announce casting requirements of the production. They may also hold open auditions, which hundreds or even thousands of hopeful actors and actresses attend to audition for parts. Most casting directors also have a file of information on all the performers who ever auditioned for them, as well as a file on those who have sent resumes and photos but never formally auditioned.

In some cases, established actors or actresses hear about a production, are interested in a specific role, and instruct their agents to call the casting director. If these well-known actors and actresses are very successful in the industry and are right for the part, they will often get a role without auditioning. Similarly, casting directors might have a specific actor or actress in mind for a part. In these instances, they contact the performer's agent to check out the interest and availability.

Often casting directors and actors meet in a "preread session." Usually, this includes about twenty people who are in contention for the part. The purpose of the meeting is to screen out people so that the producer's time is not wasted unnecessarily. From the twenty, five or six candidates might be chosen to bring to a "producer's session," which also includes the casting director.

Internships always provide invaluable education and experience. As a casting director's intern, one of your important responsibilities might be to take care of calls from producers and directors. You might also be involved in casting a TV show, which would require that you spend your days reading a script in order to determine the list of characters needed to fill these parts. Then you might send the list to agents (possibly also to Breakdown Services to forward to agents and managers), who will subsequently send you submissions (envelopes with pictures and resumes of candidates) to fill these roles. Then you'd pick out the people to audition.

AGENTS Agents are representatives who advise their clients in a certain area of expertise. They may represent athletes, writers, models, actors, producers, performers, and other types of celebrities. There are three types of agents who represent performers: commercial agents, theatrical agents, and full-service agents. Theatrical agents handle movies, TV, and stage roles. Commercial agents handle only commercials. Full-service agents handle both. Agents may also be franchised or not franchised. A franchised agent is one who is licensed to represent union performers.

Most theatrical agents work for large agencies that service many clients. They always use their contacts and are on the lookout for news about new plays or other projects so they know where and when actors will be needed.

Since it is true that an agent won't survive if his or her clients are not successful, agents may also see to it that the actors study acting, speech, voice, and dance—anything that will enhance the abilities of the clients they represent. They are definitely looking to help make their clients successful because there is a significantly larger paycheck for those whose clients strike it rich.

An agent spends most of the day on the telephone: negotiating, networking, arranging meetings, discussing prospects, maintaining connections, and keeping in touch with the industry trends and deals. Nearly one-third of all phone time is spent with clients, strategizing and explaining what the agent is doing on their behalf. Face-to-face meetings are also important. An agent has to be willing to find creative compromises and live with them. Those who are successful must have tenacity, the willingness to fight for their clients, and the ability to sell ideas effectively and communicate clearly.

GENERAL MANAGERS General managers are the individuals in charge of legal details. They may set up the play company as a corporation and also negotiate contracts with those who have been hired to be part of the production. They may aid in preparing budgets and make sure that costs stay within them. It is their job to set ticket prices, hire a company manager, and order the printed tickets.

COMPANY MANAGERS Company managers are in charge of making out the payroll and seeing to it that appropriate taxes are paid. They also work with box office managers on receipts and ticket sales. Once the show is closed, they make sure that nothing remains in the theater.

BOX OFFICE MANAGERS Box office managers are strictly in charge of tickets. It is their job to arrange the sales of tickets through mail order, advance ticket sales at the theater, and any other outlets they have in mind. They are held accountable for all ticket sales and money derived from them.

HOUSE MANAGERS House managers are responsible for the upkeep of the theater. As a result, they must be present whenever anyone else is there. They are also in charge of ushers, the observance of fire and safety laws, and the extra stagehands who are hired to move the sets into and out of the theater.

TOURING PRODUCTION MANAGERS When the show is on the road, touring production managers are in charge of all business affairs of the company. Their duties usually include obtaining local permits, hiring local stagehands, arranging for housing for the cast and other members of the staff, and working with local unions. They also audit box office accounts and write out and disburse paychecks.

THEATRICAL PRESS AGENTS Theatrical press agents are the professionals in charge of handling all of the publicity for regional theater group productions, off-Broadway shows, and Broadway shows. If a show is going to be successful, it is imperative that enough publicity is developed so that sufficient ticket sales will be generated. To accomplish this, theatrical press agents create press kits, prepare biographies, write press releases, arrange interviews, and deal with all media sources.

For this job, it is critical to make the right media contacts. This entails compiling lists that will be used to send press releases, press passes, and perhaps invitations for opening night. Along with this, the theatrical press agent must plan as many events and press conferences as possible to generate as much publicity as possible. It is important that these professionals are creative about developing new ideas and new angles for exposure through reporters, entertainment and feature writers, and other newspaper and magazine writers.

Opening night is a gala event that theatrical press agents are in charge of. It is their responsibility to call all reviewers and critics on the day of the show to make sure they will be present in the audience. The agent will be on hand on the opening day to be the liaison to the media, to pass out press kits, and to provide any information that is required.

TRAINING

Music

Though there are no specific educational requirements for many of these careers in the music business, a college degree with a broad arts and sciences background and a focus on music or at least course work in management, communications, contracts and contract law, journalism, law, business, and music is definitely helpful for success. Possessing a broad range of knowledge about music and the music industry is very important.

On-the-job training will bring the experience needed to promote you in the field. Agents who make arrangements to represent musicians or singers will get a substantial knowledge of the industry through performing in a musical group or working in a recording studio themselves. This also helps to build another important asset—contacts in the music industry—and the more, the better.

Desirable personal qualities include salesmanship; good public relations skills; the ability to evaluate and recognize exceptional talent, provide constructive advice, work well with people, gain clients and find appropriate work for them, negotiate successfully, and work at a fast pace and under great pressure; assertiveness (aggressiveness); strong communications skills; and excellent phone presence, patience, and perseverance.

For record producers, the most important ability is skill in choosing music that will appeal to many people. A number-one hit song is the greatest goal, of course. Thus, successful record producers must be so familiar and comfortable with sound and songs that they can pick songs that will do well on the charts. It is important that they can recognize raw talent, which can be cultivated and then combined with excellent arranging and high-quality recording devices.

Business managers need to be cognizant of investments and money strategies.

Acting

No standard educational or training requirements exist for producers and other theater business professionals. However, a thorough knowledge and understanding of theater is absolutely necessary, and a college degree gives individuals a certain measure of credibility and increased opportunities for hands-on training. Course work should focus on theater, film, business, English, fine arts, law, fiscal management, and personnel management. Advanced degrees are generally not necessary and, as a rule, do not affect earnings. Seminars and workshops in theater and producing are important.

Professionals in this area of theater need good business sense, financial management skills, organizational skills, effective communication skills, strong interpersonal skills, and negotiation skills. They must also have the ability to listen, to match people with roles, to work under pressure, to relate to clients, to handle stress, and to attend to details.

A three-year apprenticeship with a member of the Association of Theatrical Press Agents and Managers (ATPAM) is required for theatrical press agents. While a college degree is not a requirement, many in the business feel that it is the best approach. Good course choices include public relations, communications, writing, advertising, marketing, business, English, and theater arts. Theatrical press agents must be creative, detail-oriented, and aggressive; they should have excellent verbal and written communication skills. They need experience in publicity, public relations, or promotion.

JOB OUTLOOK
Music

The outlook for personal managers and booking agents is cautious. In most cases, individuals begin by representing local talent and work their way up to representing better-known performers. Since one agent can handle many clients, this is a competitive profession that cannot accommodate large numbers of new people. The best opportunities exist in New York City, Los Angeles, and Nashville.

Acting

The number of producers is small and few new ones are hired each year. Theatrical producers work from show to show. For agents, success lies in finding new talent and promoting it in order to earn a reputation and a bigger salary. Competition is fierce within all these occupations.

Prospective casting directors should be advised that it's almost impossible to get a job in casting without first interning. There are so many people who are willing to work for free as a way to break into Hollywood. Find out about internships by looking in *The Casting Director's Directory*, which is sold at Samuel French bookstore in Los Angeles. It lists the names, addresses, and phone numbers of all the casting directors and what shows they cast. Then send your resume.

Potential theatrical press agents should know that you can acquire much-needed experience by handling the publicity and promotion for a school, college, or community theater production. Look for seminars, workshops, and classes in publicity, writing, promotion, and theater. These experiences will improve your skills in addition to providing opportunities to make important contacts.

SALARIES
Music

Personal managers usually receive 10 to 15 percent of an artist's earnings. Often they also receive percentages of merchandise that is sold. They may earn from about $18,000 to $60,000 per year. Naturally, agents wish their clients to be successful because they usually work on a commission basis; if the clients are popular, they will make more money.

Agents for classical musicians usually receive 20 percent for their work in all fields except opera, which receives only a 10-percent commission. In many states, talent agents are licensed.

Booking agents usually take anywhere from 10 to 20 percent of the amount the act is being paid for that performance. In some cases they are paid a salary plus a percentage of the figures they add to the agency. Amounts vary considerably, but at the top they may earn anywhere from $200,000 to $750,000.

Business managers may make $20,000 to $750,000 a year or more. Earnings may be based on a percentage of the act's total gross income. The percentage varies from 3 to 10 percent.

Acting

In general, the pay for producers is good but varies according to experience, the company, and the production budget. Though producers on staff usually receive a specific salary, others do not. Instead, they might receive a finder's fee for putting together a group of investors. Others are compensated with a percentage of the profits earned from the show. Figures for producers can vary from a few thousand to hundreds of thousands of dollars. However, entry level producers in television usually earn about $20,000 per year. Unionized producers generally receive paid vacation and health insurance as well.

Because of the job's nature, it is difficult to determine annual earnings of casting directors. They depend a lot on whether professionals are consultants or on staff, the nature of the production, and how many productions they cast each year. For individuals who are on staff, salaries may range from $10,000 to $75,000 or more. Consultants may charge $2,000 to $40,000 or more per production.

Agents usually make a standard 10 or 15 percent commission of all of the client's earnings, but actual salaries vary greatly depending on the experience and talent of the individual. Agents working on a part-time basis can earn anywhere from $15,000 to $50,000 a year. Benefits also vary. Most agents working for large agencies are offered health insurance and paid vacations.

Since theatrical press agents are usually hired for specific productions, it's difficult to determine annual earnings for this work. Factors affecting remuneration include the number of projects that year, how long the production lasts, and the size and type of theater. Minimum earnings are negotiated by the ATPAM, an AFL-CIO union. Earnings include a minimum weekly salary plus vacation pay, a percentage for pensions, and a set figure for a welfare fund. Theatrical press agents usually earn about $600 to $1,600 per week and up.

RELATED FIELDS

The connections agents make in their careers come in handy if they decide to leave. Many enter the field their clients are in, such as producing, editing, publishing, and in rare cases, writing and directing. Other related professions include public relations, sales, labor relations, advertising, management, communications, and media relations.

INTERVIEW
Brian J. Swanson
Company President and Agent

With a B.S. in sociology, a B.S. in business management, and a B.S. in industrial relations from Mankato State University to his credit, Brian J. Swanson acts as president, agent, and accountant of Hello! Booking in Minneapolis, Minnesota. Previously he worked for several years in retail records, then at Capitol Records, BMG Record Distribution, Glam Slam Nightclub in Minneapolis, and Proton Productions (a booking agency) of Minneapolis.

How Brian J. Swanson Got Started

"I went into the music business fresh out of college in 1986, and started as an agent in 1992. I love the field and enjoy the fact that it offers me creative input. I am happy that I do not have to wear a suit and I am able to keep in touch with my first passion, music."

What the Job's Really Like

"Ninety percent of my day is spent on the phone with artists, record companies, or club buyers. The phone rings about sixty times a day, and it is seldom a relaxed environment. There is lots of pressure to perform, which is one of the driving forces behind the success of the company. It is seldom dangerous, unless you count high blood pressure and poor eating habits!

"I like the freedom to work with whomever I choose, provided they are interested in working with me. The hours are terrible! I work about seventy-plus hours a week in addition to the time spent at shows and on travel. The plus side is that I have become a big fish in a small Minneapolis pond. The downside is the stress. I am unsure if I want to try to swim in the big pool. I could get eaten in a day."

Expert Advice

"Advising anyone who wants to do this kind of work to *work hard* is the understatement of the year. I would advise that you make sure you have a support network financially, just in case things don't work out. Don't try to do more than one job at a time. In other words, be an agent or a manager, part of a record company or a publicist or band member. Don't try to do a couple of things because it probably won't work. You'll end up spreading yourself way too thin, and nothing will work for you. One thing is for sure: you must always keep hustling.

"Though I sometimes feel that my career can be a living hell, I absolutely love what I do."

INTERVIEW
Wayne Keller
Artists' Representative

Wayne Keller attended Michigan State University in East Lansing, Michigan, majoring in police administration and minoring in communications. He now works as an artists' representative in Nashville, Tennessee.

How Wayne Keller Got Started

"There is really no training ground or formal education for this profession. You must first learn the business from the performing standpoint, then from the producer's or club owner's angle. I personally grew up in my father's nightclub in Milwaukee, learning the entertainer's standpoint by hanging around with numerous talented performers and by utilizing normal small-business practices. Prior to becoming an agent I was an office manager for the Pinkerton Detective Agency."

What the Job's Really Like

"The most important qualifications for a new agent would be honesty, availability, and the ability to tolerate and nurture the egos of the talented. I was fortunate enough to have learned this by the time I became an agent in 1961 at the age of twenty-nine. I did not, however, have the experience that was usually almost a prerequisite for becoming an agent, namely, having been an entertainer myself. My experience was only from having been an observer of the wonderful world of show business. To my knowledge, in fact, I am the only agent who is not a former entertainer. My former wife was a performer, and she was definitely a help in handling the helm of the business (as far as staying in touch with the changing sentiments of the various acts and club owners).

"The profession is really like no other. You go out evenings to watch various people perform and endeavor to have a discussion with them. A few days, weeks, or months later they write to you (submitting photos) and advise you of their availability on a certain date. You then contact a producer or club owner and inform them of the availability of the entertainer and his or her attributes (one thing for sure is never saying anything negative about a performer you are selling). A contract for that one engagement is then prepared, and you go on to the next booking. Once you are established and have earned the confidence of both entertainers and clients with your honesty, the business becomes somewhat routine. You are the catalyst between the acts and their appearances. The atmosphere in the business is always relaxed, and you reach the point of being paid more for what you know than for the number of hours you work.

"If you're lucky enough to become nationally known and respected, the business almost amounts to making a few telephone calls and instructing your secretary to make up the contracts while you concentrate on obtaining more publicity for your performers.

"The upsides of the business are numerous if you have the ability to do the job well. You are constantly dealing with interesting, talented people behind the scenes of a fascinating field. Your income is restricted only by your own ability. Your schedule is adaptable—you need only work the hours you choose.

"The downsides include producers and club owners who are not honest with you and do not pay you the agreed-upon fees, and, to some extent, the aforementioned inflated egos of the performers. I must say, in defense of these performer egos, however, that they are a necessity. If you are to get up before hundreds of people, show after show, and night after night, you have to believe in yourself. And if your agent chooses to call that an inflated ego, it's his or her problem! For years I represented two of the greatest nightclub-style performers in the business, comedian-musician Frankie Capri and comedian-singer Nelson Sardelli. Their egos were part of their charm—and they were as good as they believed themselves to be."

Expert Advice

"If someone is interested in becoming an agent, he or she should first acquire a working knowledge of show business and then always (1) be honest and (2) be available to your people. You must realize that you are responsible for the livelihood of these entertainers, and you must take care of them as your own.

"I was attracted to the business by a love of entertainment, a fascination with the performers, and an awareness of income possibilities that superseded my career as a private detective. In working for yourself, you are totally in control of your own destiny in the business world. For me, this has translated into thirty wonderful years in this career."

INTERVIEW
Bill Hibbler
Company Owner and Artist Manager

Bill Hibbler is owner of Texas Funk Syndicate, an artist management company in Houston, Texas. He attended Houston Community College.

How Bill Hibbler Got Started

"I've spent twenty-two years in the trenches. I've dealt with vintage guitars, run sound, and handled security. I've been a backline technician, road manager, stage manager, tour coordinator, disc jockey, program director, and album project coordinator. I have also published music-industry directories, conducted seminars, and managed artists.

"I was always a big fan of music. As a child I was always the one who brought the music along. A good friend of mine kept dragging me into music stores to show me the guitar he dreamed of buying. I ended up buying a bass myself, but I was never very good at it and gave up after a while. One night after attending a concert, I spotted the salesman who had sold me my bass trying to haul about half a dozen guitar cases into the arena for the headliner's guitar player to check out. My friend and I quickly volunteered to help him carry the guitars in, and he got us each a stage pass. Once backstage, I was totally fascinated with the whole scene—meeting the bands and watching this small army of technicians and local stagehands break down the gear.

"After that, I was hooked. I spent my afternoons at the venues in the hope that I could help with the instruments or anything else. I freely offered to deliver whatever supplies the crew might need from the music store. Though I didn't make much money, I did get a couple of backstage passes to the shows and would get to meet some of my favorite bands. It wasn't easy at first. I'd have a hard time getting past security and into the arenas, but eventually I developed relationships with the local concert promoters, who realized that I was providing a service that was useful to everyone involved. By this time, most of the guitar technicians who were on the road had either met me when they'd been to Houston or had heard of me through the grapevine. I used to make sure to bring a few T-shirts and stickers along (advertising my company), and the stickers would usually find their way onto the bands' flight cases. Word started to get around.

"From the beginning, I knew I wanted to be a road manager. After graduating from high school, I went to college, but I decided to leave and instead enter the music business. During the next few years, I ran sound for local bands, booked for a small club, managed a stereo store, and worked at Houston's Agora Ballroom doing security and stage work. In 1982 I got my first break and was hired to be a backline technician for Humble Pie. After a few months there was a change in management, and I became the road manager.

"It was an unusual position to be in at the time. In those days, there were no schools that offered courses in artist or tour management careers, and it was difficult to get access to working tour managers. I'd been in contact with these professionals for years at shows, but only briefly, as they were usually very busy. I think the best way to learn this career is to find a mentor and learn what the job is really all about. However, I found myself in the job before finding that mentor. Luckily, I had pretty good instincts, which is important for anyone working on a road crew.

"I spent three great years with Humble Pie before the band broke up. A big mistake I'd made during those years was not developing a better network so that I could find more work. Usually, someone in my position would be working for a band with a big management company, booking agent, or record label that would send them out with their other bands or refer them. With Humble Pie, we didn't have that type of management, and the band wasn't signed. Our booking agent specialized in southern rock bands like the Allman Brothers, Charlie Daniels Band, and ARS, and these groups kept the same individuals, usually their relatives or friends from the early years, without hiring a new crew every time they went out (like a large number of European bands did). I couldn't find a tour manager position. So for several years I worked as a club disc jockey in Atlanta and later in Houston.

"During that time, I met Glenn Hughes when he was about to go out on tour with Black Sabbath. We became friends, and he offered me a job as his assistant on the tour. However, Sabbath's management wanted to use someone else at that time. I finally went to work for Glenn in January of 1995 as the project coordinator for his album, *Feel*. About six months later, Glenn and his Japanese record label asked me to take over as his manager."

What the Job's Really Like

"I now manage Glenn along with two local bands and am in discussions with another established artist.

"My job can be like riding a roller coaster at times. I have to wear a lot of different hats as a manager, and things are a lot more hectic some days than others. The time leading up to and during a tour is probably the busiest.

"My work schedule varies tremendously but is always centered on the telephone, fax machine, and e-mail. Glenn's primary markets right now are Europe and Japan, and due to the time difference I often find myself on the phone as early as 5 or 6 A.M. During a tour, I might finish up at 9 or 10 P.M. by dealing with our tour manager after the show. But there are often gaps in the day when I can get away for a couple of hours if there are no emergencies to deal with.

"Things are a lot more laid-back when I direct my attention to studio recording. My initial job then is to put a budget together for the album. I'll cut deals with the producer, engineer, and studios for recording, mixing, and mastering; purchase or hire any tape and equipment we'll need; and arrange scheduling and so forth. In addition to making arrangements for supplemental musicians or special guests, I'll take care of arranging photo sessions and meetings with the graphic designer to plan the artwork for both the CD and the marketing materials. (Our label lets us handle a lot of this. Other labels play a much larger role in selecting marketing materials.) During the sessions, I'll be in charge of paying all the bills and tracking expenses. As we get closer to completion, I'll be working with the label to determine promotional plans, schedules, and everything else.

"As to the downsides, I usually enjoy the challenges that arise in the United States, but I find dealing with a European tour to be pretty stressful. It's a lot easier to solve a problem like finding a piece of equipment or a replacement vehicle if the band is here in America, where you have easy access to directory assistance and everyone speaks the same language. Even something as basic as finding superglue late at night in Europe is nearly impossible (unlike in America, which has a twenty-four-hour convenience store on every corner). In addition to all the usual circumstances, you've got to deal with multiple currencies, which make for budgeting challenges and bookkeeping problems. There are increased costs of doing business in Europe; obviously phone calls are more expensive, and an overnight envelope costs four times as much to ship. In general, everything from hotels to equipment is more costly, and you have to pay value-added taxes as high as 25 percent.

"On the local scene, I've seen so many musicians who sit and complain about the city they live in or cut down a rival band that got signed, but who never take the necessary steps to make it happen for themselves. At a higher level, there are the people that can't be bothered to show up on time, do interviews, and so forth, and they step on a lot of other people's toes. They forget the old adage about people on your way up because those same people are going to be there on your way back down. Musicians like that can really be a drain on a manager.

"As far as the up- and downsides from more of a business standpoint, it's not that hard to become a manager. These days, for a few thousand dollars you can put together an office that rivals a big corporation: a computer, modem, printer, telephone, a couple of phone lines, and you're in business. Computers really level the playing field because you can handle your bookkeeping, graphic design, faxing, voice mail, trip planning, mailing lists, contact management, and marketing with one machine. With the Internet and online services, you can develop a great network, do research, and market your music without ever leaving your apartment.

"One big downside is that being a manager can become a full-time job long before it pays full-time money. Assuming a typical management commission is 15 percent, your artist has to be grossing $80,000 a year before you can earn $1,000 a month. So, it helps in the beginning to have a day job where you have the ability to make and receive phone calls at work that are band-related."

Expert Advice

"For people who might be interested in pursuing this type of work, I would suggest first of all that you read as much as you can about the business. You must acquire a feel for how recording, publishing, and merchandising deals are put together, how record companies and publishing companies are organized, and how things fit into place. You don't have to know how to operate recording and stage gear, but it helps to have a good overview of what does what and how the recording process works. And, perhaps most important, you need to learn how to understand all the various contracts you'll encounter.

"There are some excellent schools with music business programs, but many of them do nothing more than give you a bit of a foundation to build on, rather than enabling you to go right to work. The real education comes from the internship that you should serve while attending school. (If you decide to pursue the school route, I'd recommend doing so in Los Angeles or New York. In those cities you'll have a lot more access to the people who make things happen in the music business than if you choose to take a class back home.) Your school can help you with this or you can check online services, music industry forums, and magazines like *L.A. Music Connection,* which has an interns' classified section. Many of these internships require you to be in a school program, as you'll probably be working for free, and the school internship is the only way a company can get around not paying you minimum wage. That's OK at this point, because you'll be gaining valuable experience. I like the idea of interning in a smaller company, because in a major record label office, you may be stuck doing phone surveys or working in the mail room and never get to really see how things are done.

"Whatever way you choose to get a start on your education, you should treat the music business as a science. Forget the fantasy of having your band get discovered by some A & R guy who fishes your tape out of a pile of demos or accidentally stumbles into your show. Set goals, develop a plan for yourself and for your artist, and then take action.

"Besides getting an education, you want to begin developing contacts. It's never too early to start. Keep them in a software program like ACT! or Lotus Organizer or in a day-planner book. Organize your list of contacts into A, B, and C contacts, and prioritize them according to their power and position. Make A the highest level. Call your C-level contacts once every two to three weeks, your B contacts every four to six weeks, and your A contacts once every two to three months. Try to find ways to help *them* while you're trying to help yourself. Learn to be persistent, and don't let the answer 'No,' affect you personally. *No* today could mean *yes* tomorrow. Keep working on and following your game plan, making adjustments as needed. If you make a mistake, try to learn from it—and then move on.

"These days, once you've learned the business, it is entirely possible to find success no matter where you live. Get the right band with the right songs and do what's necessary to release your own CD. Before you release it, follow a preplanned promotional process, and stick to it until you've made a strong impact in your hometown. Once your act has reached that level, choose nearby cities or college towns and apply the same plan of action until you accomplish similar results. Then continue to expand city by city. Before long, you'll have a nice little region where you're getting air play at some levels, selling copies of your CD in every city, and drawing nice crowds to all your shows. Continue to expand in this fashion, and the major labels will find you.

"I love to travel, and this business gives me the opportunity to do lots of that, although you often don't get a lot of free time to explore the cities you visit. Still, it's a great adventure. Working in the music business allows me to work at home without facing the boredom of a nine-to-five type job. As a manager, I get to be a part of the big picture and work in a variety of roles. I have friends in the corporate world who are tied to a small section of a huge company. Their role doesn't allow them to see what their contribution is and their work is often duplicated by three or four other people. The tradeoff for this used to be job security. Now that is certainly no longer the case, so why not take a risk and do something you love? That's what I did!"

INTERVIEW
Gary Murphy
Publicist

Gary Murphy is an independent publicist specializing in national public-relations campaigns for the performing arts. He serves as the national press representative for the Geffen Playhouse in Los Angeles, the Alley Theater in Houston, and Santa Fe Stages in Santa Fe, New Mexico. He earned his Bachelor of Science degree in English education from SUNY at Cortland. Gary did not enter his profession overtly—it just sort of happened.

How Gary Murphy Got Started

"In 1977, while recovering from an illness, a friend suggested I tend the intermission bar at the Manhattan Theater Club in New York City as a recuperative activity. I had recently graduated from college with a teaching degree but found the idea of actually teaching unbearable. Working in Manhattan restaurants was far more appealing at the time than getting up at dawn to teach English grammar. Up until that point, my theater education was minimal: I had taken one course and seen a total of perhaps a dozen plays. It didn't really seem to be a viable career choice. MTC, lodged in the Old Bohemian Hall on New York's upper east side, had three spaces operating at the time: the Downstage had just hosted the American premiere of Athol Fugard's *Statements After the Arrest Under the Immorality Act*; the Upstage had Fugard's *Nongogo,* directed by Oz Scott and starring Mary Alice; and the Cabaret featured the world premiere of *Ain't Misbehavin'* with Nell Carter, Amelia MacQueen, and Andre DeShields. The bar was rolled into a hand-cranked elevator that opened onto the first-floor vestibule and served as intermission lobby for the two stages. It also served as elevator for the Cabaret's *Ain't Misbehavin'* cast, and I would transport them to their dressing rooms during the break. After that gig I was hooked on theater. I proceeded to work in the box office, the marketing department, and then the press department, gaining my real theater schooling in the two-and-a-half-year, paid apprenticeship at Manhattan Theater Club.

"From there I worked as the marketing and press director for Manhattan Punch Line, an independent publicist for a number of theater productions, communications director for Circle Repertory Company from 1985 to 1991, and press representative for the New York Theater workshop from 1988 to 1991."

What the Job's Really Like

"Today my everyday work routine varies from month to month. However, it always focuses on writing: memos, faxes, press releases, photo identifications, letters. I maintain a large database press list, which is constantly changed, updated, and targeted. One of my goals is to attempt to get daily news updates from clients about their projects and to collect news that can sometimes be turned into items. In addition, I hire photographers for production photo shoots and work closely with the managing directors for all theaters, taking my cues from them. When I have information in advance, I do long-lead planning and pitches. Another major responsibility is to handle all opening nights—inviting the press, creating the press kits, and meeting and greeting on the actual day. During the height of the season (October–November) all of this can translate to about sixty-hour workweeks.

"What I enjoy the most is dealing with the artists and the media. I enjoy working with writers—playwrights as much as critics—and it gives me tremendous pleasure to bring a playwright's work to the attention of the media. I have been fortunate to work with some of the finest artists appearing on stage during the last twenty years, and I've also worked with a number of vital theater institutions, responsible for keeping American theater moving forward. They include the Manhattan Theater Club, Circle Repertory Company, New York Theater Workshop, and currently the Geffen Playhouse."

Expert Advice

"Don't follow in my footsteps. Make your own way. There are no set rules, no set game plan. If you want to be an actor, designer, or director you can go to Juilliard, Yale, or Northwestern University and receive some of the best training available. Academic programs are available in theater administration, and I'd recommend that you choose one that gives you a solid liberal arts-business education along with the theater background. But more than that, if you want to work in theater these days, you just have to love it. It's that simple. Because when you love what you do, nothing is too much and the learning never stops."

FOR MORE INFORMATION

Contact the following companies for additional information about career possibilities in this field.

Columbia Artists Management
165 West 57th Street
New York, NY 10019
Contact: Human Resources

International Creative Management
40 West 57th Street
New York, NY 10019
Contact: Director of Personnel

International Management Group
One Erieview Plaza, Suite 1300
Cleveland, OH 44114
Contact: Director of Human Resources

Business managers who are accountants may join the

American Institute of Certified Public Accountants (AICPA)
1211 Avenue of the Americas
New York, NY 10036

There is an association (not a bargaining union) for personal managers called the Conference of Personal Managers, which sets standards of conduct for personal managers. Contact the following associations for more information.

Association of Theatrical Press Agents and Managers,
AFL-CIO (ATPAM)
165 West 46th Street
New York, NY 10036

Conference of Personal Managers (National)
210 East 51st Street
New York, NY 10019

International Association of Financial Planning (IAFP)
Two Concourse Parkway, Suite 800
Atlanta, GA 30328

Institute of Certified Financial Planners (ICEP)
7600 East Eastman Avenue, Suite 301
Denver, CO 80231

International Theatrical Agencies Association (ITAA)
c/o Hartland Talent Marketing
5775 Wayzetta Boulevard
Minneapolis, MN 55426

League of American Theaters and Producers
226 West 47th Street
New York, NY 10036

Music Distributors Association
38 West 21st Street, 5th Floor
New York, NY 10010

National Association of Accountants (NAA)
10 Paragon Drive
Montvale, NJ 07645

National Society of Public Accountants (NSPA)
1010 North Fairfax Street
Alexandria, VA 22314

Professional Arts Management Institute
110 Riverside Drive, Suite 4E
New York, NY 10024

Recording Industry Association of America
1020 19th Street NW
Washington, DC 20036

About the Author

Jan Goldberg's love for the printed page began well before her second birthday. Regular visits to the book bindery where her grandfather worked revealed magic combinations of sights and smells that she carries with her to this day.

Childhood was filled with composing poems and stories, reading books, and playing library. Elementary and high school included an assortment of contributions to school newspapers. While a full-time college student, Goldberg wrote extensively as part of her job responsibilities in the College of Business Administration at Roosevelt University in Chicago. After receiving a degree in elementary education, she was able to impart her love of reading and writing to her students.

Goldberg has written extensively in the occupations area for General Learning Corporation's *Career World Magazine,* as well as for the many career publications produced by CASS Communications. She has also contributed to a number of projects for educational publishers, including Scott Foresman, Addison-Wesley, and Camp Fire Boys and Girls.

As a feature writer, Goldberg's work has appeared in *Parenting Magazine, Today's Chicago Woman, Opportunity Magazine, Chicago Parent, Correspondent, Successful Student, Complete Woman,* and *North Shore Magazine,* on Arthur Andersen's Web site, and in the Pioneer Press newspapers.

In addition to *On the Job: Real People Working in Entertainment,* she is author of *On the Job: Real People Working in Communications, Great Jobs for Music Majors, Great Jobs for Computer Science Majors, Great Jobs for Theater Majors, Careers for Courageous People, Careers in Journalism, Great Jobs for Accounting Majors, On the Job: Real People Working in Science, Opportunities in Research and Development Careers,* and *Opportunities in Horticulture Careers,* all published by NTC/Contemporary Publishing Group.